MERLEAU-PONTY'S
PHENOMENOLOGY OF PERCEPTION

Merleau-Ponty's
Phenomenology of Perception

A Guide and Commentary

Monika M. Langer

THE FLORIDA STATE UNIVERSITY PRESS
TALLAHASSEE

Library of Congress Cataloging-in-Publication Data
Langer, Monika.
Merleau-Ponty's Phenomenology of perception.
Includes index.
1. Merleau-Ponty, Maurice, 1908–1961. Phénoménologie
de la perception.   2. Phenomenology.   3. Perception
(Philosophy)   I. Merleau-Ponty, Maurice, 1908-1961.
Phénoménologie de la perception   II. Title.
B2430.M3763P475   1989   142'.7   88–239
ISBN 0–8130–0892–1 Hardcover
ISBN 0–8130–0926–X Paperback

THE FLORIDA STATE UNIVERSITY PRESS is a member of University
Presses of Florida, the State of Florida's university system publishing
consortium.

ORDER BOOKS FROM University Presses of Florida, 15 NW 15th St.,
Gainesville, FL 32603.

ADDRESS EDITORIAL INQUIRIES TO The Florida State University
Press, 303 Dodd Hall, The Florida State University, Tallahassee,
FL 32306.

Available outside the United States and Canada from
The Macmillan Press Ltd., Houndmills, Basingstoke,
Hants, RG21 2XS, England.

Printed in Hong Kong

Contents

Preface

To date several commentaries have been published which deal with Merleau-Ponty's philosophy as a whole or with some particular aspect of his thought. Useful as many of these are in their own right, they do not help their readers to grapple specifically with the notorious difficulties of Merleau-Ponty's central work, the *Phenomenology of Perception*. This exegesis aims to meet that need. As Guerrière noted in publishing a translation of the analytical table of contents of the *Phenomenology of Perception*, 'the reader of the work needs all the help he can get'.[1] Even for the professional philosopher, Merleau-Ponty's text poses considerable problems because its phenomenological analyses are extremely convoluted and its style makes it difficult to distinguish the author's own position from those which he is criticizing. Merleau-Ponty's penchant for exploring related ideas and themes renders his 'argument' elusive, disjointed, and sometimes even incomplete. In addition, the text abounds in oblique references and assumes a thorough knowledge of the works of Descartes, Kant, Husserl, Heidegger and Sartre. Finally, the English translation compounds the difficulties which Merleau-Ponty's rich prose itself presents. Even the revised (1981) English edition is frequently misleading and occasionally downright incorrect; at best it lacks the nuances of the original.

My exegesis therefore reconstructs, clarifies and – where necessary – completes Merleau-Ponty's phenomenological analyses chapter by chapter. It explains the importance of various chapters and shows the logic of their sequence. Where requisite, it provides the relevant passages from the primary texts of other philosophers whose positions Merleau-Ponty is developing or criticizing, and explains just how he is doing so. Throughout, it alerts the reader to problems of translation and when necessary, re-translates key terms or passages. Finally, it considers Merleau-Ponty's own reservations about the work and offers a critical assessment of the *Phenomenology of Perception* as a whole.

In the light of the numerous difficulties noted above, the reader may well wonder whether the *Phenomenology of Perception* actually warrants the effort which is required to read it. Despite its problematic nature however, the text is a classic of phenomenology and is especially relevant today. Since the original was published over forty years ago, the latter point calls for elaboration. This introduction will serve to contextualize the *Phenomenology of Perception* and to establish its particular importance for our own time. In his PREFACE Merleau-Ponty states that 'the phenomenological reduction is that of an existential philosophy'.[2] We must therefore consider the nature of existentialist philosophy and the meaning of the phenomenological reduction.

There is a continuing widespread tendency to regard existentialist philosophy as outdated and to relegate it to the status of a brief episode in the history of modern thought. Such a view is based on the sorts of misconceptions about existentialism which Sartre addressed in his famous lecture 'Existentialism is a Humanism', delivered in the same year that Merleau-Ponty's *Phenomenology of Perception* was published. This is not the place to reiterate Sartre's defence of existentialism; rather, it will suffice to note some general points about existentialist philosophy. The latter encompasses a host of widely differing positions and no single definition accommodates all those who are generally considered its representatives. Nonetheless, a commonality of concerns underlies the diversity of these thinkers.

To detect that commonality, it is helpful to recall the marvellous story which Aristotle related about Heraclitus, and which Heidegger retold in his 'Letter on Humanism'. A number of inquisitive strangers seek out Heraclitus in hopes of witnessing something extraordinary. They are surprised to find the famous philosopher simply 'warming himself at a stove'.[3] In failing to discover anything patently divorced from daily life, the unannounced visitors are puzzled and disappointed; they are sure that a thinker warming himself at the centre of his ordinary home cannot be philosophizing. As they are on the point of leaving, Heraclitus encourages them to consider more closely the ordinary, concrete situation which they so swiftly dismissed as insignificant and irrelevant to thought. 'There are Gods present even here', says Heraclitus,[4] thereby tacitly urging his visitors to reflect on their assumption that philosophizing demands a turning aside from daily life. I am not suggesting that Heraclitus was an existentialist; however, the little story captures perfectly the core of existentialist philosophy in its emphasis on concrete thinking. In focusing on the actual human situation as the starting point for any authentic philosophy, this ancient anecdote implicitly counters the assumption that genuine thinking must be abstract. It thus stresses the central importance of pondering the meaning of our being-in-the-world and points out the general alienation from such concrete philosophizing.

Existentialist philosophy challenges the contention that philosophy is inherently high-flown; that the search for truth requires a turning away from the world of our concrete experience, as Plato's cave allegory would have us believe. It rejects the Platonic–Cartesian–Hegelian ideal of eternal truth or absolute knowledge on the one hand and, on the other, the positivistic levelling which insists on objectivity and calculation.[5] Contending that both approaches are abstract and inadequate for an understanding of our being-in-the-world, existentialist philosophy seeks to awaken us to an awareness of our fundamental involvement in a natural–cultural–historical milieu. It stresses that we are not neutral observers but rather, situated participants in an ongoing, open-ended, socio–historical drama. It claims that truth comes into being in our concrete co-existence with others and cannot be severed from language and history. The existentialists declare that a non-situated human being is inconceivable, that the philosopher does not survey the world, and that philosophy is firmly rooted in a situation which has a historical depth. Far from being the unfolding of absolute knowledge, 'philosophising starts with our situation' and attempts to illuminate it.[6] The existentialist philosophers' central concern is to prompt humans not to live thoughtlessly but rather, to have a keen awareness of their freedom and responsibility in the shaping of a situation in which they are always already involved.

The fundamental features characterizing the situation analysed by the major twentieth-century existentialist philosophers persist to this day. If we are to appreciate the particular relevance of Merleau-Ponty's *Phenomenology of Perception* for our own time, we must bear those features in mind. Already in 1931 Jaspers, drawing on Kierkegaard and Weber, published a detailed philosophical study of the deracination and functionalization of humans in mass society and warned that the attitude fostered by modern technology was profoundly dehumanizing. He stressed that 'the reality of the world cannot be evaded'; that 'the signifiance of entering into the world constitutes the value of philosophy'; and that the latter 'is not to be regarded as the objective validity of any sort of knowledge, but as the consciousness of being in the world'.[7] Following the Second World War, Jaspers focused his attention on the horrific possibilities of the new military technology and the utter inadequacy of the prevalent mode of thinking to counter the threat of total annihilation. He warned that history had become a single global movement and that the developed nuclear technology precluded any survivors in the event of another world war. Jaspers emphasized the urgent need to recognize 'that technology, know-how, achievements, are not enough', and that 'a new way of thinking' must replace the all-pervasive problem-oriented approach. Jaspers argued that only a new, non-operational 'encompassing thinking', leading to a new, non-confrontational politics, could avert a nuclear holocaust. 'If we grow sure of our freedom, and thus of our responsibility, there is a chance for . . . salvation', he concluded.[8]

Heidegger too expressed his concern about the nature of mass society, the destructive potential of modern technology, and the widespread lack of any non-operational way of thinking. He argued that 'calculative thinking' is indispensable in its proper sphere, but that it is incapable of preventing a total victimization of humans by technology. Heidegger contended that such thinking had its source in the seventeenth-century revolution in fundamental concepts, and that by the mid-twentieth century it had transformed nature into 'a gigantic gasoline station'. The same operational approach was now being applied to humans themselves, resulting in an unprecedented rootlessness coupled with the threat of a nuclear holocaust. Heidegger noted that genetic engineering was already on the horizon, but that there was a disturbing absence of thought devoted to the meaning of this utter transformation of human existence through technology. He argued that only by thoughtful questioning could the annihilation of human life be forestalled and a new rootedness established in the modern world.[9]

For their part, Merleau-Ponty and Sartre likewise criticized the prevalent mode of thinking and warned that attempts to evade the implications of the concrete situation could only lead to disaster. Thus they decided to found their famous journal *Les Temps Modernes*. In his essay 'The War Has Taken Place', which appeared in the inaugural issue, Merleau-Ponty declared: 'we have learned history, and we claim that it must not be forgotten'.[10] He urged his readers to renounce Cartesian rationalism in favour of a genuinely concrete philosophy. The latter would not take up its abode in a realm allegedly beyond the vicissitudes of daily life. On the contrary, the new way of philosophizing would elucidate the impossibility of escaping one's concrete co-existence with others, and would stress the need to participate responsibly in shaping the future.

Given the steadily increasing stockpiles of nuclear weapons, the growth of computer technology, the accelerated automation of the workplace, and the ongoing experiments in genetic engineering, the specific concerns expressed by existentialist philosophers regarding technological society are even more pressing today – and the call for a non-operationalist thinking is becoming ever more urgent. In a recent international conference on the twenty-first century held at the University of Victoria, Professor Morris Berman explicitly emphasized the need for 'a truly embodied approach to the world'. Arguing that 'we are at a crossroads now', Berman cautioned against a 'disembodied and formalistic' cybernetic thinking 'in our eagerness to reject the mechanistic science of the last 300 years'.[11] He noted that Merleau-Ponty, recognizing 'the fallacy of misplaced concreteness', warned in his 1960 essay 'Eye and Mind' that:

> Thinking 'operationally' has become a sort of absolute artificialism, such as we see in the ideology of cybernetics. . . . If this kind of thinking were to extend its reign to man and history; if, pretending to ignore what we know of them through our own situations, it were to set out to construct man and history on the basis of a few abstract indicies . . . then . . . we enter into . . . a sleep, or a nightmare, from which there is no awakening.
>
> Scientific thinking, a thinking which looks on from above, and thinks of the object-in-general, must return to the 'there is' which underlies it; to the site, the soil of the sensible and opened world such as it is in our life and for our body . . . that actual body I call mine. . . . Further, *associated bodies* must be brought forward along with my body . . .[12]

It is not difficult, especially in light of the above passage, to appreciate the exceptional pertinence of Merleau-Ponty's *Phenomenology of Perception* to our own time. As we have seen, existentialist philosophy is highly critical of any 'thinking which looks on from above'. The credibility of its critique ultimately depends upon its providing a comprehensive philosophical foundation for the latter – and that is precisely what the *Phenomenology of Perception* does. In an address summarizing and defending the work shortly after its publication, Merleau-Ponty pointed out that 'the perceived world is the always presupposed foundation of all rationality, all value and all existence'. Although 'there is a whole cultural world which constitutes a second level about perceptual experience', perception is nevertheless 'the fundamental basis which cannot be ignored'.[13] The critique of our twentieth-century cultural world as dehumanizing and destructive must therefore be based on a phenomenological account of our perceptual experience. The phenomenological reduction is indispensible for the disclosure of that primary experiential level.

If we are to understand how Merleau-Ponty employs the phenomenological reduction, we must situate his reduction within its philosophical context. Descartes had been concerned to establish the foundation for a universal science based on reason alone. He attempted to secure a method whereby fundamental self-evident truths would serve as axioms from which other truths could be deduced so as to provide an organically connected system of scientifically established truths. By submitting everything to systematic doubt, Descartes hoped to put knowledge on an absolutely firm foundation. The intuitively apprehended existence of the finite self provided the foundation – so Descartes thought – for this comprehensive scientific philosophy. However, Husserl maintained that Descartes' methodological doubt had not been radical enough. According to Husserl, Descartes' *cogito ergo sum* failed to put the *res cogitans* in abeyance. This failure to 'bracket' the 'I' as a psychological reality subverted Descartes' attempt to establish knowledge on a sure foundation, argued Husserl. At the same time, he commended Descartes for attempting to find a firm basis for knowledge by suspending all affirmations concerning the everyday world and focusing on the world as it is given to consciousness. Husserl himself therefore sought to provide an absolutely certain ground for knowledge by adopting and radicalizing the Cartesian method.

Like Descartes, Husserl began with a normative ideal of philosophy as a presuppositionless, rigorous science having universal validity and formulating eternal truths. The realization of this ideal demanded the search for a foundation, for a sphere in which things give themselves absolutely, that is, with a clarity, distinctness and completeness which renders them apodictic. Husserl's phenomenological reduction bracketed all belief in transcendent existence and focused on transcendental subjectivity – that 'I' which Kant and Husserl claimed was necessarily involved in any act of consciousness. Husserl's phenomenological reduction seemed to him to open up a realm of immanent experience capable of serving as the foundation for philosophy. This realm did not contain psychical facts, events, or experiences, as had Descartes'; rather, it consisted of universal meanings or 'essences' underlying these psychical entities. Instead of concentrating on any particular act of thinking or perceiving, for example, Husserl turned to the essence of thinking as such, or the essence of the perceiving as such.

For Husserl in short, the sphere opened up by the phenomenological reduction consisted of fundamental structures of consciousness reduced to essences – that is, to universal, absolutely necessary meanings constituted by the transcendental ego. The task of phenomenology was the descriptive analysis of these essences as they appeared to the intellectual intuition of the phenomenologist, who adopted a neutral position regarding the status of the external world. Thus the phenomenological reduction, based on the *epochē* (or suspension of judgements concerning the existential status of the objects of consciousness), was the method whereby Husserl tried to return to consciousness as the region of absolutely certain knowledge. In his *Cartesian Meditations* he asserted that the world was 'wholly constituted by the transcendental ego'. Since his philosophy dispensed with Descartes' psychical ego and showed up the presuppositions of the various sciences, it seemed to Husserl to be truly radical. The sciences, he contended, never stopped to consider what it means to observe, to perceive or to think – they presupposed these as given. It was the task of phenomenology – as Husserl conceived it – to examine such presuppositions and to describe the constitutive role of the transcendental ego. The other sciences remained naive in failing to examine their own presuppositions; with common sense, they shared the natural attitude to the world.

Towards the end of his life, Husserl began to question this 'Cartesian Way to phenomenology' and the very notion of philosophy as a rigorous science; he came to consider the transcendental ego as 'apparently empty of content'. His theory of evidence, hinging as it did on the criteria of absolute certainty and completeness, was thrown open to question by his realization that phenomenological reflection is itself temporal; that subjectively lived time is the field of all conscious acts and hence, that these conscious acts themselves unfold in time, rather than being given immediately and completely in one 'fell swoop' to a disinterested gaze. The last works of Husserl therefore began to sketch out a 'new way to phenomenology' focusing on a return to the life-world as the pre-given ground of all practical and theoretical activities. Husserl finally designated the field of perception as the very heart of the life-world. His self-criticism regarding the emptiness of the transcendental ego was taken a step further by Sartre who, in his *Transcendence of the Ego*, rejected the transcendental ego altogether.[14]

According to Sartre, Husserl was profoundly mistaken in thinking that the existing world can be bracketed. The suspension of all affirmations of existence beyond consciousness leaves only 'a great emptiness', argued Sartre, because consciousness has no contents; hence consciousness can never in fact be isolated from the existing world. The 'reduced, neutral standpoint' of the Husserlian phenomenologist therefore had to be rejected in favour of a concern with the world of our actual, lived experience. For Sartre, the reflective study of consciousness became the study of human existence situated in the world. Though constituted by consciousness, all truths, values and meanings were declared to be outside consciousness and in the world – hence they were contingent. The 'natural attitude' thus became a matter of living in 'bad faith'. In bringing to light the presuppositions of that natural attitude, the phenomenological reduction served to jolt consciousness out of its bad faith by eliminating the Cartesian–Husserlian escape-route. In the Sartrian pure reflection, 'there are no more barriers, no more limits, nothing to hide consciousness from itself'. Sartre's phenomenological reduction effectively plunges human beings 'back into the world'.[15]

Like Sartre, Merleau-Ponty rejects Husserl's abstract 'universal essences' and transcendental ego. Merleau-Ponty's emphasis, however, is on that which Husserl had designated as the heart of the life-world, namely, perception. According to Merleau-Ponty, Husserl pointed the way towards a descriptive study of the life-world, but failed to appreciate its significance. Thus the latter did not realize that the intentionality of consciousness is first and foremost a bodily intentionality. Merleau-Ponty points out that all knowledge takes place within the horizons opened up by perception, that the primordial structures of perception pervade the entire range of reflective and scientific experience, and that all forms of human co-existence are based on perception. Phenomenology's concern therefore must be with the pre-reflective world which is the background of all reflection, the world in which human beings are already engaged prior to reflection. Merleau-Ponty argues that the perceiver is not a pure thinker but a body-subject, and that any act of reflection is based on that pre-personal, anonymous consciousness which *is* incarnate subjectivity. There can be no sphere of absolutely self-sustaining thought; the only foundation for knowledge is our concrete inherence in the world. The entire universe of science is thus built upon the life-world which it takes for granted.

Merleau-Ponty criticizes the 'Cartesian Way to phenomenology' for failing to be truly radical and in fact being a 'philosophical lie'. The Cartesian philosophy falls into dogmatism by masking the origin of reflection. Consequently, a genuinely radical reflection which recognizes the pre-reflective realm from which it itself springs, is required. This 'hyper-reflection', as Merleau-Ponty calls it, does not destroy reflection for the sake of the unreflected experience; rather, it is a matter of taking account of 'the total situation, which involves reference from the one to the other'.[16] The relationship between thought and its object must be situated within that openness to the world upon which it rests. It is not possible ever in fact to undo the bond between the human being and the world, and to remake it subsequently as 'the Cartesian Way' tried to do. According to Merleau-Ponty, the task of phenomenology is to help us to see the primordial bond more clearly, to bring it to our attention. As a truly radical philosophy, phenomenology should alert us, for example, to the fact that ideas are never absolutely pure thoughts but rather, cultural objects necessarily linked to acts of expression whose source is the phenomenal body itself as already primordially expressive. In short, phenomenology must awaken us to an awareness of consciousness as incarnate in a body and inhering in a world. The notion of 'incarnate subjectivity' is therefore central to Merleau-Ponty's phenomenology.

Merleau-Ponty points out in the PREFACE that:

Seeking the essence of consciousness will therefore not consist in developing the *Wortbedeutung* of consciousness and escaping from existence into the universe of things said; it will consist in

rediscovering my actual presence to myself. . . . Looking for the
world's essence is not looking for what it is as an idea once it has
been reduced to a theme of discourse; it is looking for what it is
as a fact for us, before any thematisation.[17]

Instead of focusing on the conditions for the possibility of
experience as various transcendental philosophies have done,
Merleau-Ponty's phenomenology aims to draw our attention to
the always presupposed and actually present background of our
actual experience. It dispenses with the traditional mystifications
in so far as it refuses to regard experience as an entity which can
be analysed into its component parts, and refrains from constructing a basis for it in a transcendental sphere on the hither side of all
actual experience. For Merleau-Ponty, experience is 'a process of
transcendence'. His phenomenological reduction does not render
us the given as it appears to common sense or naive science. The
reduction subverts the reifications of the natural attitude by
showing that the given is constituted in a primordial dialogue
between body-subject and world. The given which is revealed by
this phenomenological reduction has a history and is part of a
whole network of relations; it is profoundly dynamic. Analytic
reflection and scientific induction are equally inadequate for
comprehending experience as disclosed by the phenomenological
reduction. Moreover, Merleau-Ponty himself approaches the given
obliquely, so to speak, by studying and describing the disturbances which arise from breakdowns in the primordial dialogue.

As long as that dialogue proceeds smoothly, we take its results
for granted and consider them a 'natural' world. It is when the
dialogue is disturbed that its character as dialogue begins to
emerge and we see that the subject's way of living its body is
decisive for the manner in which it apprehends the world.
Merleau-Ponty's phenomenological description proceeds in a
Hegelian fashion: at each stage of his investigation, he summons
the traditional dogmatic positions and shows how they subvert
themselves. Through the continual juxtaposition and dissolution
of these theories, Merleau-Ponty endeavours to establish that our
experience is neither a mechanistically determined process nor a
purely fortuitous construction, and that our various explicit relationships with the world are subtended by a primordial
background which cannot itself ever become entirely explicit. If
we attempt to tear our experience free from this background in

order to study it without its obscure roots, or alternatively, if we try to force that background itself to cease being a background so that we might circumscribe it completely, we only succeed in distorting that fundamental pre-personal movement of existence which are *are* and which our body continues to live despite our intellectual contortions. Ultimately, as Merleau-Ponty notes in the 'Preface', 'we shall find in ourselves, and nowhere else, the unity and true meaning of phenomenology'. As genuinely radical reflection, phenomenology recognizes that our primordial relationship to the world 'is not a thing which can be any further clarified by analysis'; the dynamic, internal relation between body-subject and world can only be brought to our attention. This bringing to attention is itself, however, a 'creative act' which brings truth into being by disclosing behind reflection that mysterious perceptual realm which is our very 'access to truth'.[18]

Before considering Merleau-Ponty's step-by-step disclosure of that pre-reflective realm, it remains for me to alert the reader to a few stylistic points and to express my gratitude to those who helped to make this book possible. Regarding the former, the reader will discover that my exegesis makes extensive use of the masculine pronoun, that my paragraphs are occasionally rather long, and that not all quotations are footnoted. After giving the matter considerable thought, I decided that it would be best to have my exegesis reflect Merleau-Ponty's own use of language; hence the masculine pronoun predominates throughout. Merleau-Ponty's particular manner of thinking found expression in extremely long paragraphs. In attempting to capture the essence of that thinking in this book, it was not always possible to avoid somewhat lengthy paragraphs myself. Since my exegesis is intended to be read in conjunction with the *Phenomenology of Perception*, I felt it was unnecessary to footnote those quotations which are drawn from the particular chapter under discussion. Finally, I would like to thank all those whose support and labour made this work possible. For their unflagging encouragement, I thank my family and friends; for their many questions and oft stated wish for such an exegesis, I thank my students; and for her unfailing good humour and unstinting labour in transforming messy inked pages into readable machine copy, I thank my secretary, Sandra Chellew. To all those who have felt frustration in grappling with the *Phenomenology of Perception*, I dedicate this book.

MONIKA LANGER

Notes

1. Daniel Guerrière, 'Table of Contents of "Phenomenology of Perception": Translation and Pagination', *Journal of the British Society for Phenomenology*, vol. 10, no. 1 (Jan. 1979) p. 65.

2. I have altered Colin Smith's translation to bring it closer to the French original, which reads: ' . . . la réduction phénoménologique est celle d'une philosophie existentielle'. (*Phénoménologique de la perception* (Paris: Éditions Gallimard, 1945), p. ix.) It is also worth noting that Merleau-Ponty equates phenomenology with 'concrete thinking' and the latter with 'what others propound under the name "existential philosophy".' (See the 'Preface' of the *Phenomenology of Perception* and pp. 133–4 of *Sense and Non-Sense* (trans. Dreyfus and Dreyfus (Evanston, Ill.: Northwestern University Press, 1964)).

3. Martin Heidegger, 'Letter on Humanism' (trans. Edgar Lohner; original published 1947) in *The Existentialist Tradition: Selected Writings* (ed. Nino Langiulli), (New York: Doubleday, 1974), pp. 237–8. My own interpretation of the story in the 'Preface' differs to some degree from Heidegger's.

4. *Ibid.*, p. 238.

5. See for example: Kierkegaard's *The Present Age*, Nietzsche's *Twilight of the Idols*, Jaspers' *Man in the Modern Age*, Marcel's *The Philosophy of Existentialism* and *The Mystery of Being*, Heidegger's *Discourse on Thinking*, Sartre's 'Existentialism is a Humanism' and *Being and Nothingness*, Camus', *The Myth of Sisyphus and Other Essays*, Merleau-Ponty's *Sense and Non-Sense, Phenomenology and Perception, The Primacy of Perception and Other Essays* and *Signs*.

6. Karl Jaspers, 'Philosophizing Starts with Our Situation', *Philosophy*, vol. I (trans. E. B. Ashton; original German published 1932), reprinted in *The Existentialist Tradition: Selected Writings*, pp. 158–61.

7. Jaspers, *Man in the Modern Age* (trans. Eden and Cedar Paul), (New York: Doubleday, 1957) pp. 194–8.

8. Jaspers, *The Future of Mankind* (trans. E. B. Ashton), (University of Chicago Press, 1961; orig. published 1958) pp. 330, 318, viii, 332, 333, vii.

9. Heidegger, 'Memorial Address' (originally given 1955), *Discourse on Thinking* (trans. Anderson and Freund), (New York: Harper & Row, 1969) pp. 43–57.

10. Maurice Merleau-Ponty, 'The War Has Taken Place', (original published October 1945), *Sense and Non-Sense* (trans. Dreyfus and Dreyfus), (Evanston, Ill.: Northwestern University Press, 1964, p. 150.

11. Morris Berman, 'The Cybernetic Dream of the 21st Century', paper presented at 'An International Conference on Social and Technological Change: The University into the 21st Century', University of Victoria, British Columbia, Canada, 4 May 1984, pp. 28–31.

    An expanded version of this paper was published (under the same title) in the *Journal of Humanistic Psychology* vol. 26 no. 2 (spring 1986) pp. 24–51.

12. Merleau-Ponty, 'Eye and Mind' (trans. Carleton Dallery) in James M. Edie (ed.), *The Primacy of Perception and Other Essays*, (Evanston, Ill.: Northwestern University Press, 1964) pp. 160–1. Quoted in 'The Cybernetic Dream of the 21st Century', p. 30.
13. 'The Primacy of Perception and Its Philosophical Consequences' (trans. James M. Edie), *The Primacy of Perception and Other Essays*, pp. 13, 33.
14. My interpretation of Husserl is akin to Merleau-Ponty's; nevertheless, many Husserl scholars would reject this reading of Husserl. For further discussion, see *Phenomenology: the Philosophy of Edmund Husserl and Its Interpretation* (ed. Joseph J. Kockelmans), (New York: Doubleday, 1967) pp. 194ff.
15. Sartre, *The Transcendence of the Ego: an Existentialist Theory of Consciousness* (trans. Forrest Williams and Robert Kirkpatrick), (New York: Noonday Press, 1957) pp. 32, 98–105 (original text published 1936–37).
16. Merleau-Ponty, *The Visible and the Invisible: Followed by Working Notes* (trans. Alphonso Lingis and ed. Claude Lefort), (Evanston, Ill.: Northwestern University Press, 1968) p. 35.
17. 'Preface', *Phenomenology of Perception*, xv.
18. 'Preface', *Phenomenology of Perception*, viii, xviii, xx, xvi.

Acknowledgements

The author and publishers wish to thank the following who have kindly given permission for use of copyright material: Routledge & Kegan Paul Ltd and Humanities Press International, Inc. for the extracts from *Phenomenology of Perception* by Maurice Merleau-Ponty, English translation copyright © 1962 by Routledge & Kegan Paul Ltd; Philosophical Library, Inc., New York, for the extracts from *Being and Nothingness: a Phenomenological Essay on Ontology* by Jean-Paul Sartre, English translation copyright © 1956 by the Philosophical Library, Inc., Washington Square Press edition published by arrangement with Philosophical Library Inc., 1966; Northwestern University Press for the extracts from *The Primacy of Perception and Other Essays* by Maurice Merleau-Ponty (English translation copyright © 1964 by Northwestern University Press), *The Visible and the Invisible: Followed By Working Notes* by Maurice Merleau-Ponty (English translation copyright © 1968 by Northwestern University Press), *Sense and Non-Sense* by Maurice Merleau-Ponty (English translation copyright © 1964 by Northwestern University Press), *Signs* by Maurice Merleau-Ponty (English translation copyright © 1964 by Northwestern University Press); Professor Morris Berman, for the extracts from 'The Cybernetic Dream of the Twenty-First Century' by Morris Berman © 1984 by Morris Berman, published in an expanded version in the *Journal of Humanistic Psychology*, vol.26 no. 2 (spring 1986).

Every effort has been made to trace all the copyright holders but if any have been inadvertently overlooked the publishers will be pleased to make the necessary arrangement at the first opportunity.

I am indebted to Ms Jude Hall-Patch for her assistance in preparing the index for this book.

I am grateful to the University of Victoria for providing timely grants to help me defray indexing and copyright permission expenses.

MONIKA LANGER

Introduction: Classical Prejudices and the Return to Phenomena

1

'Sensation'

The four chapters comprising the 'Introduction' of the *Phenomenology of Perception* are designed to provide a preliminary sketch of classical approaches to perception which will subsequently be examined in detail. In these introductory chapters Merleau-Ponty indicates why he considers the classical approaches prejudiced and why he deemed it necessary to go back to our actual experience. He also attempts to forestall possible misunderstandings regarding the nature of his own inquiry.

Merleau-Ponty begins with a critical examination of the notion of sensation. 'At the outset of the study of perception', he says, 'we find in language the notion of sensation, which seems immediate and clear.' In the course of this first chapter, that notion reveals itself to be in fact 'the furthest removed from its original source, and therefore the most unclear'. It is significant that Merleau-Ponty turns to language in commencing his study of perception. He thereby alerts us to the fact that perception is not 'a primitive function' underlying cultural acquisitions, as our 'natural attitude' would have us believe. On the contrary, what both common sense and the sciences mean by perception is itself a cultural construct which misses the phenomenon of perception.

Classical studies, Merleau-Ponty argues, have attempted to understand perception by adopting an analytical approach. This approach has resulted in the notion of sensation as the fundamental building-block of perception, and hence in the view that perception is the summation of sensations. The meaning of sensation varies according to the orientation of the theorists. It may mean the manner in which one is affected and the experiencing of a state of oneself. On such a view, sensation is an 'impression' produced in a subject; to see red, for example, is to have an impression of redness. We might think here of Locke's or Descartes' distinction between primary qualities such as extension and secondary qualities such as colour. Only the former belong to the object itself; the object is deemed not to possess colour qualities but to cause these to appear in the subject by affecting the latter in a particular way. To make colours purely subjective, however, is to render them indistinguishable, since differentiation requires a distancing – and hence, an objectifying – on the part of the subject. Pure sensation thus becomes the experiencing of an instantaneous, undifferentiated 'impact'. As such it is devoid of meaning and utterly foreign to our lived experience which, no matter how elementary, is always charged with meaning. Just as the addition of zeros never gets us beyond zero, so the summation of meaningless elements never produces a meaningful whole. Even the simplest sensory given has a figure–background structure, without which it could not *be* a sensory given. Pure, undifferentiated 'impressions' are thus imperceptible; they cannot be part of any imaginable perception. Consequently, they have no place in an analysis of perception and their retention as a theoretical construct only serves to obscure that which they are intended to illuminate – namely, the nature of perception. We will never understand perception by positing something which in principle can have nothing to do with it. The only way to learn what it is to perceive is to examine the structure of our actual perception.

In their attempt to do exactly that, many classical theorists rejected the notion of pure impression as an element of the perceiving consciousness and substituted the notion of determinate quality as a property of the perceived object. On this view, red is not a sensation, but rather a quality of something external to the perceiver. The error this time lies in making the world an 'in-itself' in which everything is determined; it is to replace one extreme with another, to move from the radically subjective and indeterminate to the radically objective and determinate. Such a move is no truer to our actual experience; instead of attending to the latter, this approach presupposes that the objects of experience are solid 'chunks' delimited by clear boundaries and separated from one another by physical voids. Perceptual experience is considered to be analogous and hence, to consist of isolated or isolable elements which are themselves clear, determinate and self-contained. This view pre-judges our actual experience of perception, dismissing in advance everything which fails to fit the model. Ambiguities are discounted on the grounds that they are due to some deficiency in the perceiver – such as inattention – rather than to a positive indeterminacy in the object perceived.

Having made quality a property of the object, empiricism (to use Merleau-Ponty's label) feels called upon to explain how that object can give rise to perceptual experience. It seems initially that common sense and physiology can come to the rescue: common sense declares that the sensory given is grasped by the senses, while physiology supplies a detailed analysis of the senses as instruments. The result is a reduction of perception to a causal process in which sensation is the immediate consequence of an excitation. The perceiver becomes a physical system undergoing physico–chemical stimuli and responding in determinable ways. Atoms of matter stimulate the sense organs, and the stimulation is transmitted via the central nervous system to the brain where it is recorded and deciphered to produce an experience corresponding to the stimulus. Minute particles of colour qualities, for example, are thus claimed to be at the origin of the experience of colours; hence the notion of sensation as instantaneous impression seems to have been reinstated on a firm physiological footing – even if only as an explanatory concept.

Physiology itself has in fact, however, been forced to renounce its claim to have found an anatomical path connecting the stimulus to the perceptual experience. Such a model is incapable of accounting for the blatant lack of correspondence between stimulus and phenomenon which characterizes so much of our actual experience. Variations in pitch having to do with a sound's intensity, the perceived inequality of lines objectively equal, the grey resulting when red and green are presented together, the change to a less differentiated structure following injuries to sight are all cases in point. Merleau-Ponty therefore argues that that which is perceived by its very nature admits of ambiguity and belongs to a context – or 'field' – which shapes it. Hence we must reject all attempts to decompose perception into sensations and to reconstruct experience out of determinate qualities. We must abandon the belief in an external world in itself, which all the sciences share with common sense. Instead, we must return to the pre-objective realm if we are to understand what it really means to see, to hear and to feel.

2

'Association' and 'Projection of Memories'

In the previous chapter Merleau-Ponty pointed out the problems encountered by those who invoke the notion of sensation in analysing perception. Even the simplest sensory given, as we have seen, must have a figure–background structure, and such a structure is irreducible to that absolute coincidence of the perceiver with an impression or quality which defines sensation in its classical sense. In order to be perceived as a figure, that which is perceived must stand out from a background, it must have a contour, an outline. If that outline were merely another sensation, it could not *be* an outline. We are then tempted to think that it must be a collection of atomic sensations viewed simultaneously. Thus we conceive the outline as a line, and the latter as the sum of indivisible points having no intrinsic connection themselves. But what makes the sensations arrange themselves in this way before us, and why do we say that we are seeing a red patch? The standard answer is that we recognize this particular distribution of sensations because we have seen similar distributions in the past and have learned to use the words 'red patch' with reference to them. This response, however, is itself open to the same question; hence, it has merely served to defer the problem rather than to resolve it.

If sensory givens are themselves devoid of meaning, then something must be invoked which will endow their summation with the meaning of 'patch'. Empiricism assumes that the appeal to association and the projection of memories will supply such meaning. However, as Merleau-Ponty notes, these operations not only call for a consciousness for which empiricism cannot itself account, but they also presuppose that which they are supposed to explain. What could possibly prompt the perceiver initially to make of a conglomeration of 'pure impressions' the seeing of a triangle, for instance? If we are not to become entangled in an infinite regress, association and memory must themselves be grounded in a perceptual experience which is already inbued with meaning. There must be something about the present perceptual data which prompts the perceiver to put into play a certain association, or call up a certain memory. The present perceptual data therefore cannot themselves be meaningless; for such neutral 'building blocks' could never have any power to evoke others. A certain arrangement of lines on a paper is seen as a triangle *because* it itself has the same meaning as the figure which we formerly learned to call 'a triangle'. If this were not so, there would be no reason why a past experience of a circle rather than a triangle should not be called up. There must be something about the present data which guides the evocation of memories.

The appeals to association and memory presuppose the present recognition of a figure; consequently, association and memory cannot serve as explanatory principles in the analysis of perception. Nor can the empiricist thesis of sensation be retained if our experience is to be comprehensible. If we accept the idea that we have sensations, we commit ourselves to the view that all experience is sensation, as even the apprehension of spatial or temporal relationships must then be analysable into sensations. Knowledge itself becomes no more than the anticipation of impressions, and is itself constituted of such 'inexpressible impressions'. The segregation of our perceptual field into identifiable things and spaces becomes no more than the unstable configurations of extrinsically related qualities assembled by some inexplicable 'associative force' operating according to the contiguity and resemblance of stimuli. Things have no inherent substantiality as *things*, and owe their unity entirely to a consciousness – itself unaccounted for – which constructs them on the basis of past experience. Once again, this merely transfers the problem from the present to the past; that which prompts us to recognize something as a *thing* in the first place, remains incomprehensible.

By clinging to the notion of sensation, we render ourselves incapable of going beyond it; we reduce the whole of experience to 'blind processes' consisting of mechanical recordings of, and reactions to, arbitrary arrangements of meaningless units. To add that these present processes are based on similar processes in the past, in no way makes them any less opaque. Consequently, we must discard the theory of sensation and the postulates constructed to salvage it. There *is* no 'associative force' which operates autonomously as an efficient cause of experience; and the alleged 'projection of memories' is simply 'a bad metaphor' which obscures both the immanent meaning ['sens'] of the immediate experience and the manner in which the past is present to it.* The thing perceived is not a conglomeration of sensations and memories, the latter projecting themselves independently upon the former. By returning to phenomena, we discover 'a whole already pregnant with an irreducible meaning'; and it is this whole, rather than the alleged sensations and memories, which forms the 'basic layer' of all experience. The problem is thus no longer, as for empiricism, one of explaining how the projection of a recollected former arrangement of meaningless sensations can render a similar grouping of present sensations meaningful. Rather, it now becomes a matter of describing the way in which an inherently meaningful present experience at every moment has access to a past which 'envelopes' it. The relationship between past and present must therefore be re-examined, and Merleau-Ponty indicates that the past will need to be described as a 'horizon' or 'atmosphere' or 'field', instead of as a collection of discrete impressions or qualities. He concedes that this description will be quite foreign to empiricism and that the latter can always resist accepting it. Merleau-Ponty's discussion of this point is important, as it is intended to forestall misunderstandings about the status of his phenomenological investigation of perception.

Empiricism rejects as obscure and inadequate the evidence – such as the horizon of the past – revealed by phenomenological reflection. Instead, it insists on a theoretical reconstruction of such evidence in terms of impressions, which it regards as the ultimate constituents of experience. Since any and all phenomena are immediately subjected to the same sort of reconstruction, none can serve to disprove empiricism. In general, one cannot refute thinking which rests on the prejudice of the objective world, by describing phenomena. As Merleau-Ponty points out, to those already committed to an objectivist approach, physical or psychological or intellectual atoms will invariably seem more real than the phenomena of experience. Nevertheless, for the phenomenologist our experience is 'the ultimate court of appeal'. Rather than refutation, Merleau-Ponty therefore sees his task as being one of

---

* I am retaining Merleau-Ponty's distinction between 'sens' and 'signification', by altering the translation where necessary.

attempting to make thought aware of itself. This will mean awakening it to its own prejudice and to an appreciation of perception as the first access to things and the foundation of all knowledge. As justification for the phenomenological approach, Merleau-Ponty points to the wealth of hitherto inaccessible phenomena which become comprehensible once it is adopted. Yet, as Merleau-Ponty acknowledges, empiricism can always object 'that it *does not understand*' such phenomenological descriptions. The only recourse for the phenomenologist is 'to point out everything that is made incomprehensible by empiricist constructions and all the basic phenomena which they conceal'. The subsequent three parts of the *Phenomenology of Perception* will provide this sort of 'inventory'; hence Merleau-Ponty contents himself with a short preview of major points here.

We have already seen that empiricist constructions of perception deprive things of their inherent substantiality and unity by depicting these as the products of a consciousness which operates according to association and projection of memories. Now Merleau-Ponty draws our attention to the fact that empiricst constructions similarly deprive 'the "cultural world" or "human world"' of its intrinsic cultural or human meaning – thereby destroying its substantiality as a *cultural* or *human* world. The perception of a co-worker's emotions or the distinctive atmosphere of a particular city becomes merely the products of transferences and projections of memories by 'an "acosmic" thinking subject'.

Moreover, by reducing the natural world to a sum of stimuli and qualities, empiricism falsifies it too, and gives us under the guise of 'nature' what is in fact a cultural object. Empiricist constructions make incomprehensible the *presence* of the perceived world – and the loss of that presence for the hysterical child. While retaining the kernel of truth in empiricism, reflection will need to reconsider 'the whole problem of the *presence* of the object'. The natural and the cultural world will need to be rediscovered and described. As that description progressively unfolds in the subsequent chapters, the inadequacy of empiricist constructions will become increasingly evident.

3
'Attention' and 'Judgment'

At the beginning of this 'Introduction', Merleau-Ponty already pointed us ahead to the present chapter by noting that 'the notion of attention . . . is no more than an auxiliary hypothesis, evolved to save the prejudice in favour of an objective world'. In the preceding chapters, Merleau-Ponty criticized that prejudice in his attack on empiricism. Now he proceeds to show that despite its appearance to the contrary, intellectualism shares the same prejudice and is equally incapable of accounting for our perceptual experience.

Empiricism takes the objective world as given and argues that this world must impinge causally on the perceiver: the sense organs are stimulated in such a way as to receive and transmit data which are then somehow decoded by the brain so as to reproduce a picture, or 'image', of the original external stimulus. This theory involves the 'constancy hypothesis', according to which there is 'in principle a point-by-point correspondence and constant connection between the stimulus and the elementary perception'.[1] As we have seen, however, this theory fails to account for the discrepancies between the apparent and the real size of objects, for the perception of grey resulting from the presentation of red and green together, and so on. The sensory given thus defies its definition 'as the immediate effect of an external stimulus'.[2] Instead of rejecting the presupposition of a world in itself, empiricism attempts to save this prejudice by appealing to additional factors.

To account for those cases in which the percept obviously does not correspond to the stimulus, empiricism therefore invokes the notion of 'attention'. It argues that the 'normal sensations' are present in all cases, but that they occasionally remain unperceived because of lack of attention to them. Like a torch, attention can be focused on the sensations to illuminate them. Why attention occurs in some cases but not in others – why some stimuli 'trigger off ' the 'searchlight' while others do not – remains unexplained.

10

If the relationship between perception and attention is an external one, then the question involves us in an infinite regress because that which 'triggers off ' attention must itself be 'triggered off ' by something else, and so on *ad infinitum*. Since empiricism has only external relationships at its disposal, attention remains inexplicable. Just *what* attention adds to the data so as to render confused or illusory perceptions clear and viridical, is a mystery. As a purely general power, or 'searchlight', attention presumably does not create anything new in the data. Consequently, the elementary perception already contains the structure required to make it an image of the external object. In that case, how can it appear confused? Moreover, since it deals with sensations, empiricism is at a loss to account for this *structure* of perception – a structure which emerges only with attention.

In an effort to make of this incomprehensible empiricist position something intelligible, psychologists turned to intellectualism. Thus they argued that the constituting activity of consciousness creates the structure of that which we perceive, and that this structure is there whether or not we believe that we see it. Once again, attention merely illuminates what is already present; and if it is asked what is given prior to the structuring activity of consciousness, the answer is 'chaos' or a Kantian 'noumenon'. Attention does not involve a progressive clarification because there is no indistinctness – there is only chaos or clarity. But as Merleau-Ponty points out, if consciousness by its very activity produces structures, it must possess them; hence, it becomes incomprehensible how it can ever be deceived about anything. Attention thus seems unnecessary, and illusions defy explanation.

By the same token, contingency is ruled out; there is no accounting for our experience of exploring something, of learning about the things which we perceive. If consciousness itself creates perceptual structures, then it must already have them as soon as we perceive what we take to be an object – hence there is nothing more to explore or to learn. Nevertheless, our own experience tells us otherwise. When we see something indistinct, we attempt to make it more distinct by paying attention to it. In this case, we are initially neither totally ignorant nor totally cognizant of what it is we are seeing; yet empiricism in effect postulates the former while intellectualism postulates the latter. Both rule out any indeterminacy by their dogmatic adherence to that 'natural attitude' shared by common sense and the sciences – an attitude which takes the existence of an objective world to be self-evident, either 'as a reality in itself' or 'as the immanent end of knowledge'. [Empiricism] offers us a world in itself which impinges causally on the perceiver. [Intellectualism] counters this absolute objectivity with an absolute subjectivity which merely duplicates the empiricist world by a consciousness conceived as sustaining it. Both approaches simply construct experience so as to fit their presuppositions; neither is capable of grasping the 'living nucleus of perception'.

Psychologists themselves began to challenge this dogmatic belief in the world in itself, with the discovery that patients suffering from certain disorders whose origin lies in the central nervous system, cannot clearly locate a point on their body which is being touched – yet they are not totally ignorant of it either. What we have here is 'a *vaguely located spot*' which overturns the empiricist and intellectualist notion of attention. In addition, Merleau-Ponty points out that when infants begin to distinguish detailed colours where formerly they perceived ' "warm" and "cold" shades' or, even earlier, 'the coloured' and 'the colourless', what has changed is the *structure* of their perception, the *articulations* of their visual field. It is not, as psychologists claimed, that the infants in fact saw determinate colours all along but merely failed to pay attention to them. Attention is best understood on this model because, as Merleau-Ponty notes, paying attention is not merely elucidating pre-existing data. Attention progressively articulates what is initially given as positively indeterminate, as a 'still ambiguous meaning'. There is at the start neither absolute chaos nor perfectly distinct qualities; nor is there complete transparency at the end of this development. Attention is creative, but its creativity is *motivated* by what is initially only 'an indeterminate horizon'.

These points will be discussed in far more detail by Merleau-Ponty in the body of his *Phenomenology of Perception* of course; the introductory section merely serves to sketch out the directions which the subsequent phenomenological description will follow. In the same manner, Merleau-Ponty here mentions the experimental manipulations which make of attention the act of looking through a cardboard tube or telescope. Such manipulations fundamentally distort our usual perceptual experience, by presupposing a fully determinate and precise world which is then brought about artificially. Believing that this 'sleight of hand' must not go unchallenged, Merleau-Ponty here reiterates that 'consciousness must be faced with its own unreflective life in things and awakened to its own history which it was forgetting: such is the true part that philosophical reflection has to play, and thus do we arrive at a true theory of attention'. We must not presuppose that the analytic reflection employed by intellectualism will lead us back to that unreflective life just because it goes contrary to the naive realism of the empiricist position. Merleau-Ponty is concerned to show that both miss the mark.

As we have seen, neither empiricism nor intellectualism is able to assign any comprehensible role to attention. Given the constancy hypothesis, it is not difficult to see that something is needed to link up the isolated qualities impressed upon the sense organs, so as to produce an image of an object rather than a host of discrete points. Not only can it provide just the sort of co-ordinating function required here, but the faculty of judgement also seems to be able to supply an explanation of illusions and more generally, of any discrepancies between our retinal images and the perceived object. When, for example, we declare that we see people on the street below our window even though we objectively see nothing but hats and coats, intellectualism explains that in fact we do not really *see* people below, but merely *judge* that they are there. Perception thus becomes an intellectual *construction* which uses bodily impressions as primitive data to be interpreted, elaborated, or used as premises for the further activity of drawing a conclusion. In this way, all sensing experience becomes an activity of judgement – all seeing or hearing becomes a judging that we see or hear 'x'. This, however, runs contrary to our actual experience, in which there *is* a distinction between sensing and judgement. Intellectualism cannot account for the fact that a face or a landscape seen upside down is unrecognizable. It is this sort of experience which dictates the abandonment of the constancy hypothesis. If we adopt intellectualism, the distinction between 'true' and 'false' perception cannot ultimately be upheld. Since seeing means thinking or judging that we see, it is nonsense to say that the sufferer from hallucinations *thinks* he sees something which he does not really see. After all, to say he sees it is – on this theory – already to say that he thinks he sees it; hence we are forced to conclude that he thinks he sees what he does not think he sees. If one argues that the sufferer from hallucinations draws unwarranted conclusions – that he judges in the absence of adequate premises – the problem is merely pushed one step back. It will still be necessary to explain how we are to distinguish between those impressions which are adequate and those which are not. This will force the classical theories to acknowledge the existence of an immanent significance ('signification') in the elementary sensible – and that is precisely what they have already ruled out.

The efforts to save the prejudice in favour of an objective world create irresolvable dilemmas for both empiricism and intellectualism. Merleau-Ponty will show that far from being the primordially given, sensory givens are the product of a scientific approach to perception. We get no further if, like Kant, we focus on the conditions for the possibility of perception or if, like the early Husserl, we turn to the abstract essences of perceiving, thinking, and judging. All these approaches rest on a dogmatic belief in a determinate universe and in an absolute truth. The overthrow of 'the naturalistic notion of sensation' already implies the ruin of analytic reflection which had adopted it; and as Merleau-Ponty reminds us, it is the task of philosophy to embark on the 'authentic' or 'radical' reflection foreshadowed in the collapse of the classical theories. This phenomenological reflection will need to return to, and elucidate, the 'perceptual origins' of our actual experience instead of situating itself in the midst of a 'ready-made world'. Such a new approach will require concepts (like *motivation*) which are 'fluid' enough to express a domain that is neither 'objective' nor 'subjective', where being is not fully determinate and significance not entirely clear. Merleau-Ponty admits that Cartesians will dismiss this new approach as lacking philosophical import. Its vindication will require a theory of reflection in which the facticity of consciousness is shown – so that thought becomes cognizant of its inability to cut itself loose from perceptual experience in order to grasp itself absolutely. The chapter 'The Cogito' will address itself explicitly to this task.

4

The Phenomenal Field

In this final chapter of his 'Introduction' Merleau-Ponty retraces briefly the major points which have emerged in the previous chapters, discusses the need for the type of phenomenological description which the subsequent chapters will provide, and summarizes the direction which the latter will take.

By making sensing the possession of an inert quality, empiricism reduced the world to a spectacle and our own bodies to mere mechanisms. Sensing thereby lost that vitality, that mysterious richness, which it in fact has in our common experience. Empiricism rendered incomprehensible the primordial, pre-reflective significance which the world has for us as incarnate subjects, which makes of that world not a spectacle but 'a familiar setting of our life'. It has therefore become necessary to reconsider the nature of sensing and to tackle the problem of describing it as 'that vital communication with the world', that 'intentional tissue' which underlies and sustains all thought. Sensation, attention and judgement as constructed by the classical philosophies can no longer be accepted; the emergence of significant groupings can no longer be reduced to a *de facto* co-existence or an intellectual connection of meaningless impressions. Perception can no longer be collapsed into knowledge; nor can the creating of connections remain the perogative of the understanding. The prejudice of the world in itself must be abandoned and, with it, many of the concepts and distinctions employed by the classical philosophies. A new dimension calling for new conceptions is thus opened up, and Merleau-Ponty designates it 'a *phenomenal field*' to indicate that it is not a spectacle spread out before a disembodied mind, but rather an 'ambiguous domain' in which perspectival, incarnate subjects are situated. It is in this domain that perceptual experience can be rediscovered.

What place should this perceptual experience be assigned *vis-à-vis* scientific knowledge on the one hand, and psychological and philosophical reflection on the other? Merleau-Ponty contends that 'science and philosophy have for centuries been sustained by unquestioning faith in perception'. Beginning with a preconceived idea of the world and a corresponding ideal of knowledge, science considered perception as providing access to that world and so paving the way for scientific knowledge. Consequently, instead of examining our actual perceptual experience of phenomena, science interpreted it with reference to the theoretical constructs of pure bodies endowed with statistically determined chemical properties and free from any force. Geometrical space and pure movement – both lacking any internal relationship to objects – replaced our lived experience of space and motion, while events became the result of determinable physical conditions. Objects were divorced from their relationship to any particular perceiver and thereby stripped of all perspectivity, ambiguity or indeterminacy. At least in principle, they were fully determinate and identical for all perceivers, thus ruling out any irresolvable contradictions within subjective or intersubjective experience. Since perception was not regarded as a dialectical process in which something comes into being, reflection considered a genealogy of being unnecessary. Moreover, the being which science defined became the only conceivable being, irrespective of the value assigned to the principles of science. As a result, the living body became an object like all the others, equally reducible to physico-chemical properties and causal relations. Emotions and attitudes were translated into impressions of pleasure and pain, and the latter linked to processes of the nervous system. Similarly, gestures and actions were resolved into objective movements explicable in terms of nervous functioning. Sensing became a matter of stimulus–response: the body, reduced to an object, mechanically received, transmitted, and reproduced qualities of the external world.

Since the living body has ceased to be the visible expression of our being-in-the-world and become instead a machine, subjectivity lost its anchor and became a disembodied consciousness surveying the world. Perception of others and co-existence with them became impossible. Since the body of the other, like our own, had been converted into an automaton, we could at best *infer* the existence of another consciousness which, like ours, was disembodied (and hence lacked particularity). But this meant constituting the other consciousness – thus reducing it to the status of an object in our world. Solipsism was unavoidable and the consciousness of the scientist became the universal constituting subject for whom the entire world lay spread out. In short, intersubjectivity and perception collapsed into solitary thought; the self dissolved into the transcendental subject. Having accepted uncritically the fundamental assumptions of classical science, reflective philosophy found itself equally incapable of assigning any status to the empirical self.

Scientific advances – such as those in quantum mechanics – and the experience of two world wars undermined the classical approach. Einstein's relativity theory and Heisenberg's uncertainty principle challenged the classical dichotomy between a fully determinate world in itself and an impartial human observer. Space and time lost their absolute independence and an inherent uncertainty replaced the absolute determinability of nature. The classical assumption of an absolute standpoint was no longer tenable; the perceiver's situation could no longer be ignored. Nature ceased to be a spectacle; the perceiver became a participator and science found itself forced to tolerate a measure of indeterminacy. The notion of 'a *truth in itself*' had to be abandoned in favour of a truth relative to a human knower. Science was compelled to discard its pure concepts and reflective philosophy, which had shared the same assumptions, had to follow suit. Moreover, these theoretical challenges were strengthened by the chaos of war, which overturned the classical conception of intersubjective life. As Merleau-Ponty shows in his moving essay 'The War Has Taken Place', the concrete experience of barbarism shattered the very premises of rationalism. Irresolvable ambiguities and contradictions could no longer be ruled out; human society could no longer be regarded as 'a community of reasonable minds'; history could no longer be dismissed as unessential. The actual experience of irrationality and unfreedom revealed the contingency of reason and liberty, showing their dependence on particular forms of human co-existence. Rationalism lost its alleged universality and became a philosophy rooted in a specific historical context which it ignored on principle. Similarly, the absoluteness of classical science was shattered, disclosing the latter as 'a form of perception' which considered itself complete simply because it conveniently forgot its own origins. It is therefore essential that we break with uncritical perception and the classical presupposition of determinate being; that we go back to our actual experience of the world and rediscover the dialectical process of living experience whereby we ourselves, other people and things come into being. Merleau-Ponty designates this reawakening of perception and rediscovery of phenomena 'the first philosophical act'.

Merleau-Ponty cautions, however, that returning to phenomena does not mean embarking on introspective psychology nor intuitionism. Phenomena are not 'states of consciousness', nor is the phenomenal field an 'inner world' accessible to the individual subject alone. Merleau-Ponty's own position must not be confused with that of the psychologists who in challenging the validity of analysing experience in terms of physical concepts, nonetheless retained the presupposition of the objective world. They merely constructed, inside that world, a realm of 'psychic facts' and 'psychic energy' corresponding to the physical facts and mechanical energy assumed to exist outside the psyche. Since extension characterized physical data, non-extension became the trait of their psychic counterparts. Lacking extension, the latter were perceivable only by an act of intuition which was by definition private and non-communicable; impressions were beyond the reach of philosophical reflection. By contrast, the return to phenomena restores our lived experience of intersubjectivity and establishes the foundation for authentic philosophizing. The criticism of the constancy hypothesis involves the rejection not only of sensation but also of the theory of consciousness based on it – which Ryle so aptly described as 'the dogma of the Ghost in the Machine'.[3] Consciousness is then no longer constructed of impressions and the apprehension of 'mental life' – our own and that of others – ceases to be a matter of 'some inexpressible coincidence'. The dichotomy between 'internal' and 'external' experience disappears and, with it, the conception of 'mental life' as a mysterious 'inner' counterpart of 'outer' behaviour. The immediate is no longer a meaningless atom of psychic life, but rather the very structure of behaviour – our own and others' – which is a whole saturated with immanent significance. Others' 'mental life' thus becomes immediately accessible in the unfolding of their behaviour, rather than having to be inferred by introspection. Moreover, introspection ceases to be a privileged surveying of alleged 'states of consciousness' and becomes instead a rendering explicit of the meaning immanent in any behaviour. Once we reject the notion that consciousness is a psychic entity encased in a machine, the body ceases to be a barrier to consciousness and becomes, on the contrary, that which makes others immediately present to us in living experience.

In breaking with the psychological atomism of introspective psychology to describe the Gestalt's irreducible meaning, Gestalt psychology made a significant advance. However, Merleau-Ponty criticizes its tendency to treat consciousness as an assemblage of 'forms' and to adhere to the ideal of an explanatory psychology. He warns that uncritical acceptance of Gestalt psychology can lead once again to the distortions of classical transcendental philosophies. Psychologists' reflection on the primacy of phenomena prompts them to consider these as constituting the objective world. From there, it is but a small step to the postulating of a universal constituting agent – the solitary thinking ego – which constitutes not only the objective world but also that of living experience. The phenomenal field thus turns into a transcendental field; unreflective experience loses its fundamental facticity to become a mere anticipation of reflection and the latter achieves complete self-transparency. In short the world, other people and we ourselves as individuals all collapse into a Hegelian Reason, while the dogmatism of idealism replaces that of empiricism. Even Husserl's transcendental phenomenology as described in works dating from his last period presents this absorption of 'the "lived-through" world' into the transcendental ego. Despite its claims to the contrary, such an approach is ultimately uncritical. In countering it, Merleau-Ponty reminds us of the meaning of *phenomenology* and transcendental *field*.

Phenomenology does not study the actualizing of a pre-existing reason or the conditions for the possibility of a world. Rather, as the word itself indicates, *phenomenology* studies the appearing of being to consciousness. Moreover, in deliberately employing the word *field*, phenomenology emphasizes the irreducibility of the world and the perspectivity of reflection. Reflection thus understood is not the surveying of a world spread out as a spectacle for a disembodied, all-encompassing Thinker. It is, rather, an activity of an individual philosopher and is always conditioned by the latter's concrete situation in the world. If it is to be truly radical, phenomenological reflection will need to reflect on itself, maintain a constant awareness of its own source in an unreflective experience and recognize that it invariably transforms that unreflective experience in submitting it to reflection. Philosophy becomes authentically transcendental, or radical, by questioning the *pres-*

umption that reflection can, so to speak, 'catch itself by the tail' and make knowledge completely explicit. As Socrates understood so well, philosophy's core 'lies in the perpetual beginning of reflection, at the point where an individual life begins to reflect on itself'. There is thus no unbridgeable chasm separating naive consciousness from radical reflection; however, 'the prejudice of the objective world' makes the naive consciousness forget that living experience in which both it and philosophical reflection are rooted. Stripped of psychologism, the psychological description of the phenomenal field can provide a bridge by reviving perceptual experience and thereby eventually inducing consciousness to embark on a radical reflection.

Notes

1. *Phenomenology of Perception*, p. 7.
2. Ibid., p. 8.
3. Gilbert Ryle, *The Concept of Mind* (Harmondsworth, Middlesex: Penguin, 1976) p. 17.

Part I
The Body

Experience and
Objective Thought:
the Problem of the Body

As we have seen, objective thought takes the form of realism ('empiricism') or idealism ('intellectualism'). In this prefatory section, Merleau-Ponty outlines how it is that 'objective thought' arises at all and how space, time, and the body figure in such thinking. He also points out the need for a description of 'the emergence of being' which will show that objective thought is a mere moment of experience rather than its foundation. Since our perception leads to objects, we tend to overlook the origin of these objects – the fact that they have their source 'at the very centre of our experience'. Thus we neglect the crucial part which we incarnate subjects play in the constitution of the objects of our perception, in their coming into being *as objects* for us. Instead of recognizing our own role, we consider them to be objects in themselves. Alternatively, we go to the opposite extreme by distorting our own contribution in perception so as to make of it a power of creating *ex nihilo*. In this way we overlook the fact that while objects *are* 'for us', they are so only as 'in-themselves for us'. Objects are not mere projections or constructions of our minds; rather, they are objects to be encountered or discovered. In short, they are things offering a certain resistance to our touch and a depth to our gaze.

To indicate how we are tempted into the modalities of objective thought, Merleau-Ponty invokes the example of perceiving a house. We see the house next door as we walk past it to our own: we see it first from the one side as we approach it, then from the front as we pass it and finally from the other side as we walk up the path to our own door. If we were to enter our neighbour's backyard, if we were to go in his front door and see the inside of his house, or if we were to fly over his roof in a helicopter we would see the house differently. Since the house is seen differently from one angle than from another and since we are nevertheless aware of seeing the same house from different positions at different times, rather than six different houses, we all too easily conclude that it *itself* is an 'in-itself ' – that it exists independently of any perspective. However, such realism subverts itself as soon as we pause to consider its implications. If the house *itself* is indeed independent of any perspective then it must be a house 'seen from nowhere' or, what amounts to the same thing, seen from all possible perspectives simultaneously; but that involves a contradiction in terms. To see is, after all, 'always to see from somewhere'; hence the house allegedly 'seen from nowhere' or 'seen from everywhere' cannot be *really* seen – it must be invisible. Yet as we were prompted to attribute autonomy to the house *itself*, we continue to claim that it exists. Consequently, we have a house which, though invisible, nonetheless exists; it must then belong to the realm of ideality rather than to that of reality. The house *itself* is now no longer a spatio-temporal thing but an idea. By a curious reversal, the naive realism with which we began has transformed itself into a full-blown idealism. Merleau-Ponty therefore sets himself the task of tracing both these positions back to their origin in experience.

As we have seen, the perspectivity of vision was what prompted us to posit the house *itself*. Given that we could see the same house from different places at different times, we were led to conclude that the house *itself* exists independently of any perspective. In this brief introduction, therefore, Merleau-Ponty begins to examine the spatio-temporal structure of perception. The key concepts in this examination – perspective, field and horizon – are internally related. The adopting of any particular perspective can take place only in a perceptual field and that field, in turn, is a field only insofar as it has horizons. When we perceive a house, we perceive it perspectivally and, as we have seen, by taking up any particular position from which to view it we imply the possibility of taking up others. In short, the house lends itself to exploration and invites our gaze to move around it. We can comply only insofar as the house is part of a certain 'setting' whose ultimate horizon is the world. The latter is the 'horizon of horizons', the general setting of all perceptual experiences. In our example of the house, the *particular* horizon may be the street, the town in which it is located or the surrounding countryside. These are what Merleau-Ponty calls the 'outer' horizons of the house; correlatively, the 'inner' horizons enable our gaze to explore the interior of the house from a variety of positions. However, we cannot simultaneously 'open up' the outer and inner horizons of the house; focusing our gaze on any particular object inevitably means allowing the others to retreat to the fringes of our visual field to become part of the background. These surrounding objects nonetheless continue to count in our vision and we are free to draw any one of them into the foreground if we choose to let the object of our present focus retreat to the periphery. Thus we are never imprisoned in a particular perspective; nor need we fear that our concentration on any particular object will entail the others' loss of identity. Moreover, those others have horizons in which the object of our present focus is implied, thereby guaranteeing that this object too will retain its identity while we explore its various aspects. Such exploration is not an intellectual operation and there is no need to know anything about the eyes' retinal structure for it to occur. Nor is there any need for explicit recollection or conjecture, since the object's identity is not constructed from images.

Identity implies temporality; therefore the 'object-horizon structure, or the perspective', is not merely spatial but spatiotemporal. As such, it has an inherent openness which makes it impossible for an object of experience ever to be absolute – for that would require the compressing of an infinity of different perspectives 'into a strict coexistence'. This notion of 'an absolute object' is based on the perspectivism of experience; but in bringing in the idea of the co-existence of an infinity of different perspectives, we destroy temporality – and thereby the very experience underlying the notion of an absolute object. In place of that experience, this sort of thinking substitutes a reconstruction based on 'the prejudice of the objective world'. In this 'freezing' of experience the living body is reduced to an object among other objects. Yet our body is in fact the *sine qua non* of perceptual experience and we thus encounter considerable difficulties in regarding it as an object. Conversely, the objectification of our body is decisive in bringing the objective world into being; hence the collapse of the former leads to the downfall of the latter. To restore 'the perceiving subject as well as the perceived world', Merleau-Ponty therefore begins the *Phenomenology* proper with a critical examination of 'the body as object and mechanistic physiology'. When the body becomes our 'point of view upon the world' instead of an object, the spatio-temporal structure of perceptual experience will be revived and objective thinking in general undermined. The problems posed by objective thought will lead us to recognize the body as a *project* rather than an in-itself. Further, such a recognition will necessitate a re-examination of those perceptual objects which form the goal of the bodily transcendence. The result will be a radical modification in the subject–object structure implicit in the very notion of a 'project'.

1

The Body as Object and Mechanistic Physiology

Objective thought, as we have seen, posited a world of objects in which different objects as well as different parts of the same object were related in a purely external manner. Mechanistic physiology incorporated the living body into this causal system by converting human behaviour into a pattern of stimulus–response. Thus the stimulus was thought to impinge on a particular sense organ which in turn transmitted sensations to the brain and thereby produced a predictable perception. However, neural physiology found itself forced to abandon this purely mechanistic approach when it became evident that damaging centres or conductors resulted in subjects' loss of discrimination – frequently progressive – among stimuli rather than in an outright loss of 'certain qualities of sensation or of certain sensory givens'. What was at stake in such injuries was the organization of the sensory fields, the modification or collapse of figure–background structures. Consequently, modern physiology itself replaced the mechanistic stimulus–response model with the notion of an organism which meets and relates to stimulation in a variety of ways. Since the stimulation of a sense organ did not in and of itself invariably produce a perception, it became necessary to speak of an 'attuning', or disposition, of the organism to the excitation and to regard perception as a 'psychophysical' rather than a purely physical and physiological event. Nonetheless, adopting this more sophisticated 'psychophysical' model did not necessarily mean discarding causality and third person processes altogether. There was a tendency to regard the organism's shaping of stimuli as the product of an objective body whose internal organs send messages to the brain. Our experience of the body was thereby reduced to a 'representation' or 'psychic fact' resulting from objective events occurring in our 'real body'. Thus the model which began with a confusing mixture of physical and psychological factors – excit-

27

ation and 'attuning' – ended by collapsing the alleged psychological aspect of the event back into complicated physiological
processes. In doing so, it ultimately encountered the same
problem which it had been designed to resolve – namely, the
problem of inadequacy in accounting for actual experiences.

To illustrate the shortcomings of the traditional views, Merleau-
Ponty discusses the phenomena of the phantom limb and anosognosia. A strictly physiological account fails to explain how a
limb which in fact is no longer physically part of the body can
nevertheless be experienced and, alternatively, how a limb which
has become paralyzed can be systematically left out of account
even though it is still part of the body and has not actually become
anaesthetized. Nor can a purely psychological account elucidate
the phenomena, since it cannot explain why the phantom limb
disappears when the nerves to the brain are cut, or how the
anosognosic evades his handicap without simply forgetting it or
failing to see it. It must be remembered here that Merleau-Ponty's
criticisms throughout the *Phenomenology* are directed against
'empiricism' and 'intellectualism'. The psychological account
which is under attack above belongs to the intellectualist approach
and seeks to explain phenomena in terms of the presence or
absence of determinate mental contents. The phenomenon of the
phantom limb is indisputably bound up with the personal history
of the subjects in question, since such a limb can come into being
through emotions or circumstances recalling those in which the
injury occurred. Nonetheless, emotion and recollection are not to
be understood as intellectual operations here but rather, as pre-
objective ways of relating to the world. Similarly, the personal
history is irreducible to a collection of memories or brain 'traces',
since that would preclude the disappearance of the phantom limb
in the absence of brain injuries (which would presumably damage
or destroy the brain's alleged contents).

Explanations in purely physiological or purely psychological
terms evidently cannot account for phenomena such as anosognosia and the phantom limb. Yet such phenomena can be related to
both physiological and psychological conditions; consequently, it
would seem that we could arrive at an adequate explanation by
mixing these conditions. However, such a hybrid theory likewise
remains fundamentally unsatisfactory. If we begin with a radical
distinction between the 'physiological' order on the one hand and
the 'psychic' on the other, any subsequent attempt to establish an

intrinsic connection between the two is bound to fail. Given the complete antithesis between a being which is purely 'in-itself' and one which is exclusively 'for-itself', any meeting point is utterly inconceivable. Such a point of contact would require a combination of the essential features of being-in-itself and being-for-itself; yet this sort of combination has already been ruled out in the very positing of these two fundamentally opposed kinds of being.

Descartes' unsuccessful struggle to establish the union of body and soul (or mind) remains the most famous of such attempts to amalgamate mechanistic being and translucent consciousness. Since the Cartesian position is also the clearest instance of what Merleau-Ponty refers to throughout the *Phenomenology* as 'intellectualism', it is worth presenting Descartes' view in some detail at this point. Descartes '[begins] by observing the great difference between mind and body. Body is of its nature always divisible; mind is wholly indivisible'.[1] He notes that 'although the whole mind seems to be united to the whole body,' if one loses a limb one is 'not aware that any subtraction has been made from the mind'.[2] Thus Descartes is led to assert 'the total difference between mind and body' and to 'observe that [the] mind is not directly affected by all parts of the body; but only by the brain, and perhaps only by one small part of that – the alleged seat of common sensibility'.[3] Moreover,

> since any given disturbance in the part of the brain that directly affects the mind can produce only one kind of sensation . . . man as a compound of body and mind cannot but be sometimes deceived by his own nature. For some cause that occurs, not in the foot, but in any other of the parts traversed by the nerves from the foot to the brain, or even in the brain itself, may arouse the same disturbance as is usually aroused by a hurt foot; and then pain will be felt as [though] it were in the foot, and there will be a 'natural' illusion of sense.[4]

That Descartes himself recognized the inadequacy of this account is evident from his correspondence with Princess Elizabeth. In writing in response to the latter's request for clarification regarding the soul's power of moving the body, Descartes acknowledges that he has 'said almost nothing' about it and tries again 'to explain . . . the union of soul and body and how the soul has the power of moving the body'.[5] That explanation consists of no more than the observation that the union in question is a 'primitive notion' and that the soul's way of moving the body is to be conceived by analogy with gravity.[6] When Princess Elizabeth replies that she finds this response incomprehensible, Descartes can only answer that 'the similie of gravity. . . . is lame', that 'the human mind is incapable of distinctly conceiving both the distinction between body and soul and their union, at one and the same time'; and that 'finally, it is just by means of ordinary life and conversation, by abstaining from meditating and from studying things that exercise the imagination, that one learns to conceive the union of soul and body' because 'what belongs to the union of soul and body can be understood only in an obscure way either by pure intellect or even when the intellect is aided by imagination, but is understood very clearly by means of the senses'.[7] Despite repeated attempts to do so, Descartes clearly found himself unable to reconcile his 'ordinary life' experience with his philosophical view of the relationship between body and soul. The former forced him to admit 'that I am not present in my body merely as a pilot is present in a ship; I am most tightly bound to it, and as it were mixed up with it, so that I and it form a unit'.[8] Descartes' 'meditating' prompted him to 'consider the human body as a machine fitted together and made up of bones, sinews, muscles, veins, blood and skin' as opposed to 'a conscious being; that is a mind, a soul (*animus*), an intellect, a reason'.[9] Having recognized 'only two *summa genera* of realities: intellectual or mental (*cogitativarum*) realities, i.e. such as belong to a mind or conscious (*cogitantem*) substance; and material realities, i.e. such as belong to an extended substance, a body', Descartes necessarily failed to establish 'a close and intimate union of body and mind'.[10]

Traditional attempts to explain the phenomena of human experience in purely physiological or purely psychological terms have shown themselves to be inadequate, as have those approaches which, like Descartes', merely sought to mix the two kinds of explanations while leaving both fundamentally intact. Consequently, such efforts must be abandoned for a phenomenological description which situates human existence *between* the 'physiological' and the 'psychic'. It is this sort of description which Merleau-Ponty himself endeavours to provide. By way of a preliminary step in this direction, he points out that even in reference to the non-human order the 'physiological' has traditionally been conceived far too narrowly. At the level of the insect for example, it is blatantly ridiculous to speak of phenomena such as 'repression', 'refusal to accept mutilation' and the like. But here too we cannot account for the phenomena if we regard the insect's body as an object obeying the laws of mechanistic physiology. Mechanistic physiology will never explain the insect's substituting a sound leg for a severed one but not for a leg which has only been tied. Although there is here no conscious substitution aiming at some goal, there is no purely automatic substitution either. Even at this lowly level therefore, it is necessary to describe the body – the insect's in this case – in a way which transcends the traditional alternatives of 'physiological' and 'psychic'.

We must discard the well-entrenched idea that reflexes are 'blind processes'; instead, at all levels of life we must speak of a certain manner of 'being-in-the-world'. In the case of the insect, of course, it is a matter of 'an *a priori* of the species and not a personal choice', since insects of the same species all respond to mutilation in roughly the same way – whereas at the human level the response is much more varied and complex. In both cases, however, bodily injury brings to light what can only properly be called a 'global' or bodily *intentionality* having to do with a pre-objective 'orientation towards a "behavioural setting" '. Insofar as it is a pre-objective view, being-in-the-world is equally irreducible to either of Descartes' 'two *summa genera* of realities' – pure thought or extended being; as a result, being-in-the-world can unify the 'physiological' and the 'psychic'. It does so by reintegrating them into existence in such a way that 'they are no longer distinguishable respectively as the order of the *in itself*, and that of the *for itself*, and that they are both directed towards an intentional pole or towards a world'.

By invoking the notion of being-in-the-world, we are able to comprehend the ambiguity which characterizes such phenomena as the phantom limb and anosognosia. It is no longer a question of a stock of 'representations' still present after the amputation of a limb or unaccountably absent despite the persistence of a limb which has been crippled. Further, since the subject can describe the peculiarities of his phantom limb, he cannot be unconscious of its existence; yet his awareness of it does not prevent his attempting to walk on the missing leg. For the subject, the awareness of the missing or the crippled limb is not 'clear and articulate' but rather, 'unclear', ambiguous. As Merleau-Ponty notes, the subject

who continually substitutes his right arm for his crippled left arm
does not engage in deliberate decision-making. Rather, he continues to project himself through his body towards his habitual
world. From this phenomenological perspective, bodily experience is not reducible to an actual momentary interoceptivity
occurring in a particular instant of the present. The amputee's
phantom leg and the anosognosic's paralyzed arm bring to light a
bodily temporality which is not of the order of 'objective' time.

The body is seen to comprise 'like two distinct layers', the
'habitual body' and the 'present body'. The former signifies the
body as it has been lived in the past, in virtue of which it has
acquired certain habitual ways of relating to the world. The
'habitual body' already projects a habitual setting around itself,
thereby giving a general structure to the subject's situation. Since
it outlines, prior to all reflection, those objects which it 'expects' to
encounter at the other pole of its projects, this body must be
considered an 'anonymous', or 'prepersonal', global intentionality.
As such, it draws together a comprehensive past which it puts at
the disposal of each new present, thereby already laying down the
general form of a future it anticipates. With its 'two layers' the
body is the meeting place, so to speak, of past, present and future
because it is the carrying forward of the past in the outlining of a
future and the living of this bodily momentum as actual present.
This is why the anosognosic continues to perceive objects as being
manipulatable for him although his handicap precludes his mani-
pulating them any longer. Similarly, by projecting his customary
situation around him, the amputee's habitual body may prompt
him to try to walk on his missing leg. Usually, subjects gradually
accept their disability as they build up a modified habitual body.
The latter then ceases to project the formerly habitual setting to
which those subjects are now no longer able to respond effectively. As Merleau-Ponty notes, the very fact that their habitual
body – at least initially – continues to outline a 'customary world'
in which they can no longer act in their habitual way, continually
reveals their handicap to them. Yet that awareness need never be
made explicit; it may well remain paradoxically present and
absent simultaneously. Thanks to their customary body, subjects
may remain indefinitely open to a future which has in fact been
ruled out by their injury. Inasmuch as their daily activities were
not preceded by reflection in the past, no reflection is now

required to keep their customary world 'alive' – and no explicit awareness will automatically bring about its collapse.

Experiences like those of anosognosics or those of persons with phantom limbs – or, in general, those of patients with any of a whole variety of complexes – bring to light the temporal structure which characterizes our existence as incarnate beings. The psychoanalyst's patient typically suffers from a 'complex' – such as a particular phobia – whose origin lies in a traumatic experience in that patient's past. Because the experience was so painful for him, the patient 'repressed' his 'conscious' awareness of it, thus banishing the memory of his experience into the 'unconscious'. Although ousted from consciousness, the experience thus continues to exist at the unconscious level and from there overshadows and poisons the patient's present. He thus remains the prisoner of his past, so that the structure of his subsequent experience is frozen even though its content changes. In order to release him from the clutches of his past, the psychoanalyst typically prompts the patient to bring the experience back into conscious awareness and by analysing it, to purge it of its traumatic aspect. Thus the patient is finally able to leave the past experience behind him and become genuinely open to his actual present.

This haunting of the present by a particular past experience is possible because we all carry our past with us insofar as its structures have become 'sedimented' in our habitual body. There is thus an 'organic repression' which is part of our human condition and which constitutes so to speak 'an inborn complex'. This 'organic repression' underlies any more specific repression of the type discussed above. To the extent that it is rooted in biological existence, our personal existence is inherently precarious; yet we hide this precariousness from ourselves by mostly repressing the organism and reducing the past to a collection of ideas or images. Such phenomena as the phantom limb can reawaken us to the actual character of the past and thus to an appreciation of the role which our body plays in our being-in-the-world. Since emotion and memory can bring about the phenomenon of the phantom limb, it is evident that the patient is experiencing 'a former present' rather than merely recollecting it or having an idea or image of it. The phantom limb is therefore analogous to the repression of a traumatic experience discussed above; in both cases the subject remains emotionally involved in a particular past experience to such a degree that it imposes itself on the actual present. By reopening time memory evokes a certain past, inviting us to relive it – rather than simply to imagine or rethink it. In responding to this implicit summons, the amputee can cause his missing limb to appear as 'quasi-present', but this phenomenon is not to be construed as involving either a 'physiological' or a 'psychic' causality. Instead, it is a matter of the patient's taking up an 'existential attitude' which 'motivates' the appearance of the missing limb. The fact that the patient can no longer 'call up' the limb if his afferent nerves are cut, confirms the extent to which being-in-the-world is based on bodily existence. As we have seen, however, bodily existence is not reducible to the laws of mechanistic physiology but is itself imbued with meaning by our being-in-the-world. Consequently, it is not a question of joining a soul to a mechanistic object, as Descartes tried to do, but of recognizing the dialectical movement of our existence.

That movement ceaselessly carries anonymous biological existence forward into personal existence in a cultural world and conversely, allows the personal and the cultural to become sedimented in general, anonymous structures. This sedimentation is essential insofar as it frees us from the necessity of having to pay strict attention to every single thing we do, no matter how simple it may be. We thereby attain the 'mental and practical space' that enables us to build a personal existence and a human world. On the other hand as we have seen, the acquisition of general structures by the habitual body opens the possibility of our becoming fixated in a past experience. Thus the dialectic of freedom and dependence is part and parcel of the dialectical movement which characterizes our existence as incarnate beings. Since traditional approaches have distorted our existence by reducing it to mechanistic physiology or to intellectualistic psychology, Merleau-Ponty endeavours to restore its dialectical nature by showing up the inadequacies of such approaches. Having examined existence via physiology in this chapter, he proceeds to consider it by way of psychology in the next.

Notes

1. Descartes, 'Sixth Meditation', *Meditations on First Philosophy* in Elizabeth Anscombe and Peter Thomas Geach (trans. and eds), *Philosophical Writings* (London: Nelson and Sons Ltd, Nelson's University Paperbacks for The Open University, 1970) p. 121.
2. Ibid., p. 121.
3. Ibid., p. 121.
4. Ibid., pp. 122, 123.
5. 'Letters illustrative of Descartes's Philosophy 1630–1647 ', *Philosophical Writings*, pp. 274–5.
6. Ibid., pp. 275, 276, 277.
7. Ibid., pp. 277–82.
8. 'Sixth Meditation', *Philosophical Writings*, p. 117.
9. Ibid., p. 120; 'Second Meditation', *Philosophical Writings*, p. 69.
10. 'Extracts from *Principles of Philosophy* illustrating Descartes's Use of certain Terms and his Principles in Physics', *Philosophical Writings*, pp. xlviii, 190, 191.

2

The Experience of the Body and Classical Psychology

Classical psychology's own characterization of the body indicated crucial structural differences between the latter and objects; yet because of their commitment to the standpoint of an impartial observer, psychologists failed to appreciate the philosophical significance of these fundamental differences. Classical psychology recognized, for example, that the body itself has a permanence which is unlike that of objects. We establish an object's permanence by exploring it from diverse perspectives in space and time and determining whether it persists throughout the exploration. Moreover, an object can be removed from our perceptual field altogether. We cannot, however, detach ourselves from our body; hence we can neither take up various perspectives on it nor dislodge it from our perception. In short, our body is permanently present for us without our ever being able to observe it like an object; the angle from which we perceive our body is unalterable. Yet this permanent and invariable presence of our body is what enables us to observe objects; it is the prerequisite for the latters' variability and potential absence. Once again, the dialectical relationship between freedom and dependence comes to light: we have the freedom to choose and to vary our perspective on objects only on the condition that we cannot do the same vis-à-vis our body. There can *be* objects for us only because our body is not itself an object for us; our body's permanent presence is a metaphysical necessity if objects are to be physically present and relatively permanent for us at all. Consequently, the difference between the perspectivity and permanence of the body on the one hand and objects on the other is not a difference in degree but rather in kind. It is not a question of the body being *more* permanent in the sense of impinging on the receptive nervous

36

system all the time whereas objects would do so only some of the time. The body's permanence is primordial and the lack of it inconceivable. Similarly, the body's perspective constitutes our bond with the world, our fixed opening onto it, rather than one among many perspectives seen from some ideal standpoint outside the world. In short, were it not for the permanence and perspectivity of our body, the relative permanence and the perspectivity of objects would be utterly inconceivable.

Merleau-Ponty acknowledges that we can see some parts of our body with our eyes, that mirrors enable us to see ourselves from top to toe as well as from the rear, and that we can even see our own eyes by using a mirror. Nevertheless, this does not refute Merleau-Ponty's claim that we cannot observe our body as we can an object, because even a three-way mirror does not enable us to keep our body fixed while changing our point of view. Moreover, we cannot perceive our body perceiving; we can touch with one hand the other while the latter touches something else, but the activity of touching cannot itself be touched. The touched hand is not our hand actually engaged in touching something; nor are the eyes seen in the mirror our own eyes in the process of exploring the world. As Merleau-Ponty notes, we can neither see nor touch our body 'in so far as it sees or touches the world'. Although we can regard a part of our body as an object, its active being thereby escapes us.

Classical psychology recognized our body's peculiar power to give us 'double sensations'; it noted that the body can *almost* catch itself in action as it touches or sees. Our hands pressing against each other rapidly alternate back and forth between touching and being touched, while our eyes looking at the mirror see themselves 'from the outside' as it were and likewise alternate between looking and being looked at – yet the active and passive roles of our body never completely coincide. Moreover, as Descartes already conceded, our relationship with our body is not like that of a ship's pilot who observes the condition of his ship. We *feel* pain *in our foot* when we step on a nail – we do not regard the hurt foot as an external object which acts on our nervous system so as to produce an external impression. Accordingly, in its description of the body, classical psychology distinguished the latter from 'external things' by noting 'that the body is an affective object'. In addition, this psychology invoked the notion of 'kinaesthetic sensations' to indicate the difference between moving our body and moving external objects. If we decide to move a particular book from the shelf to our desk we must first locate the book, reach for it, grasp it and transfer it from its former position on the shelf to its new place on the desk. By contrast, we have no need to locate our arm and hand in order to reach for the book; our decision to reach is immediately implemented since our body is not an external object to be located and grasped like the book. With the term 'kinaesthetic sensations' classical psychology sought to express this immediate awareness in which bodily movements are executed without the need of any intermediate steps to link intention and action.

The description which classical psychology gave of our body thus already assigned it a special status; nevertheless, psychologists either failed to distinguish our body from objects or saw no philosophical implications in making such a distinction. Typically, their detached approach led them to regard the fundamental differences between objects and the body as no more than contingent peculiarities of our experience. The experience of our body they reduced to the status of a representation – a psychological fact corresponding to the physical facts studied by the other sciences. Unlike the other scientists however, the psychologists were ultimately studying their own experience in examining our experience of the body. Consequently, they were inevitably led back from experience as a representation – an object – to experience as a phenomenon, that is, as our pre-objective presence to our body and to the lived-through intersubjective world. In short, despite their attempt to consider human experience as an object, the psychologists' implicit awareness of their own subjectivity invariably interferred with their spectator's attitude. They were the subject and object of their own study and this equivocal status of being both observer and observed obliged them to rediscover the lived relationships underlying and anterior to any subject–object differentiation. By noting the distinctive features of the body, classical psychology thus unwittingly pointed the way for a 'return to experience'. In the following chapters Merleau-Ponty will examine in more detail the features of our body which prompted this return.

3

The Spatiality of the Body Itself and Motility*

In the previous chapters we saw how the problems encountered by mechanistic physiology and the observations made by classical psychology prepared the way for a phenomenological description of the body. Merleau-Ponty now pursues that description with an investigation of spatiality, since 'the primary condition of all living perception' is spatial existence.

Our experience shows that the parts of our body are not related to one another as objects occupying a place in objective space. It would be bizarre to speak of one arm as being eighteen inches to the left of the other, or of our head as being three feet above our knees. In performing an autopsy on a corpse, we might regard the latter as a collection of limbs and organs, but we do not experience our body as being such an assemblage. If for some reason we regard our body in the manner of a corpse or of an intricate machine, such a view remains entirely abstract; it is no more than an intellectual construction or a manner of speaking which leaves untouched the lived presence of the body itself. The body is immediately present to us because we *are* our body; but how is this immediacy to be understood? We know where our limbs are without having to look for them, because we possess 'a *body image*' which includes them all. The meaning which Merleau-Ponty gives to this notion, however, needs to be distinguished from that assigned to it by traditional psychology.

Initially psychologists used the term 'body image' to designate the habitual associations of images accompanying various stimuli and bodily movements. Built up in the course of recurrent expe-

---

* It should be noted that Merleau-Ponty used the word 'motricité' rather than 'motilité'; nevertheless, I have decided to follow Colin Smith in translating 'motricité' as 'motility', since the alternative 'motority' is so uncommon. However, I have translated 'le corps propre' as 'the body itself ', since this captures Merleau-Ponty's meaning better than does 'one's own body' or 'the personal body'.

riences, the body image was a *de facto* totality of impressions
which indicated the location of local stimuli and the position of all
parts of one's body at every instant. Thus understood, it was
inadequate to explain disorders such as the referral of sensations
to the wrong part of the body or the phenomenon of the phantom
limb. Psychologists themselves were therefore prompted to go
beyond the associationist definition of the body image to invoke
the notion of 'a comprehensive bodily *purpose*', thereby rendering
the body image inherently dynamic. In the psychologists' investigation of the phantom leg and the paralyzed arm, it became clear
that the body image can include a limb which has become actually
non-existent or omit a limb still extant. The decisive factor in such
cases was the *project* in which the subject felt engaged; hence the
body image proved to be irreducible to a mere copy of the
objective body or to a global awareness of its existing parts. The
psychologists themselves failed, however, to draw any philosophical consequences in implicitly developing this notion of the
body image as incarnate intentionality. It was incumbent on
Merleau-Ponty therefore to take up the developed definition of the
body image and point out its philosophical implications.

The implicit change in the notion of body image from a mosaic
of associations to one's awareness of the body as incarnate
intentionality, implies a crucial shift from the body as object to the
body as experienced. The latter – the 'lived body' – cannot be
divorced from the world as experienced, because the notion of
incarnate intentionality already implies the pole of that global
bodily purpose. As the setting of actual and potential tasks to be
accomplished, the world cannot be left out of account; it is the
horizon always already outlined in the very manner in which the
body exists. Underlying the various particular projects which I
implicitly or explicitly set myself is the comprehensive pre-
personal project of the body as being-in-the-world. The latter
gives my particular personal projects their style and they in turn
play their part in shaping it. The body image provides me with a
pre-reflective knowledge of the location of my limbs, but this
location is not a position in objective space. Rather, it is a location
with reference to the way in which my limbs enter into my
projects; thus it is not 'a spatiality of position but a spatiality of
situation'.

The lived spatiality of the body as an organic unity polarized by
tasks, constitutes the basis of that objective space which has to do

The body as experienced = the lived body

with external coordinates and determinate positions such as 'front', 'back', 'bottom', 'inside', 'outside', 'left' and 'right'. As Merleau-Ponty showed in earlier chapters, perception is always perspectival and has to with figure–background structures. To see is to see from somewhere, and this 'where' can be described as a position of the objective body with reference to external objects. Thus I see the house across the street from my kitchen window for example, and my position in my kitchen can be specified precisely; yet it is the lived body which enables me to take up such a position in objective space. It is this phenomenal body which makes the house stand out for me against the background of the sky or, alternatively, enables me to shift my gaze to a bird flying across my visual field so that the bird momentarily becomes the figure while the house recedes to form the background. Since it is the very condition for the possibility of figure–background structures coming into existence for me at all, the lived body cannot itself be another one of these structures. Hence it is what Merleau-Ponty calls 'the third term, always tacitly understood, in the figure–background structure, and every figure stands out against the double horizon of external and bodily space'. Bodily space envelops my limbs in such a way that I know where they are without having to think about them or look for them. Moreover, my awareness of my body is inseparable from the world of my perception. The things which I perceive, I perceive always in reference to my body, and this is so only because I have an immediate awareness of my body itself as it exists '*towards* them'. The body image thus involves a primordial, pre-reflective *orientation* and *motility* insofar as I am immediately aware of *where* my limbs are as my body *projects* itself towards the world of its tasks. I am always already situated in the world and it is my manner of engaging in particular projects which reveals most clearly the nature of my bodily spatiality. An analysis of motility consequently serves to elucidate the phenomenological description of spatial existence.

Normally we take for granted the basic 'power of projection' which forms such an integral part of our pre-reflective experience. Indeed, the nature of this fundamental motility tends to elude us if we concentrate exclusively on the behaviour of normal subjects. Merleau-Ponty therefore turns his attention to an examination of pathological motility in order to illuminate our usual mode of orienting ourselves in the world. Gelb and Goldstein's case study of Schneider provides a convenient starting point for the discussion of impaired motility. Since being injured at the back of the head by a shell splinter, Schneider has suffered from a whole variety of disorders including visual, motor and intellectual disturbances. His visual data are unstructured, 'almost amorphous patches' among which he distinguishes people from cars for example, by the fact that the former look longer and thinner. In order to recognize things, Schneider must sketch in their contours by moving his body in various ways. He has no difficulty performing concrete movements such as blowing his nose or cutting the leather which he uses in his job as a wallet manufacturer, and can do these things even with his eyes closed. Nevertheless, he cannot form any image of objects not actually in sight, and has great difficulty in performing abstract movements (such as raising his arm on command) if ordered to keep his eyes shut. Schneider succeeds in performing these movements 'which are not relevant to any actual situation' only if he is allowed to watch his limbs or to engage in preparatory movements involving his entire body. He cannot describe the position of his limbs, identify characteristics of objects placed against his flesh or determine which part of his body is being touched; yet he has no problem slapping a mosquito which bites his chin. If ordered to point to his chin, Schneider can comply only if allowed to grasp it. His various difficulties make it clear that there must be a difference between 'bodily space as the matrix of [one's] habitual action' and bodily space as a determinate place in the objective world.

Schneider has a body image in so far as he goes about his daily activities without having to search for his limbs, and can immediately slap a mosquito without reflecting or needing to locate either his chin or his hand in objective space. Here he directly experiences his chin as itching and his hand as having the potential to assuage the itch; hence he has not entirely lost the pre-reflective awareness of his body as a power, as incarnate intentionality. For his daily tasks, his familiar setting serves to mobilize his limbs; the customary concrete situation calls for certain movements in the interest of the task to be performed, and the phenomenal body responds with its habitual gestures. Yet curiously enough, Schneider does not feel himself to be the author of his activities; instead they seem to him to be 'triggered off ' by the situation. As he says, he experiences himself and his movements to be merely 'a link in the whole process' of events. When at rest, his body is a formless mass. Not only abstract movements but imaginary situations pose tremendous problems for Schneider, precisely because he does not experience his body as a 'power of action'. Thus although he clearly understands what he is to do, he cannot 'convert the thought of a movement into actual movement'. His only recourse is to set his body in motion blindly until distinctions take shape in its 'amorphous mass', bringing his limbs into objective existence for him and fortuitously producing an approximation of the requested gesture. As indicated earlier, one's experience of the body goes hand in hand with one's perception of the world. For Schneider, both body and world are essentially congealed, thus ruling out any creativity on his part. He cannot project himself beyond the actual so as to organize the world in light of a personal goal; for him everything is experienced as ready-made. He succeeds in grasping a part of his body or cutting leather for his job because unlike abstract movements, these remain within the realm of the given. The crux of Schneider's illness lies in the collapse of that crucial power of 'projection' which is rooted in one's experience of the body as a 'motor project'. Schneider therefore lacks that specifically 'human space' which enables us to envisage possibilities, create meanings, and shape our situation.

Merleau-Ponty takes care to point out that morbid motility – and illness in general – is a total way of being-in-the-world. Hence the difference between Schneider and healthy persons is not to be found in some characteristic or set of facts. Any causal explanation, moreover, merely obscures the phenomenon. Although his illness is of course linked to his occipital injury, Schneider's morbid motility is not a matter of an intellectual or physiological defect. He not only understands the various orders but is also anxious to comply, and his success with concrete activities makes it evident that there is nothing physiologically wrong with his eyes or limbs. Yet even in his habitual tasks, as we have seen, Schneider never feels that he is acting freely; on the contrary, he experiences his actions as being determined by the world. Despite not having to look for his limbs in performing these customary activities, Schneider in effect regards them as third person processes when prompted to consider them under questioning. As we have seen, abstract movements are purely intellectual notions for Schneider and then, as he struggles to actualize them, they become for him simply third person processes performed by his body apprehended as an object in objective space. Normal persons, on the other hand, neither feel coerced in concrete movements nor require laborious mental deductions and blind physical motions to perform abstract movements. They are open to abstract and imaginary situations. Their body image has a 'horizon of possibilities' because they experience the body as a 'motor intentionality'; and for them every movement is inseparably consciousness of movement and movement. It is not a matter of a positional consciousness of the world and the body, but of a motor significance which 'speaks to' their body. Their pre-reflective experience of the body as a 'power of action' enables them to transcend the given and structure their world in accordance with personal plans, or to lend their body freely to the realm of the imagination. Normal persons, in short, project around themselves that human space which Schneider lacks.

Neither empiricist nor intellectualist psychology is able to elucidate this fundamental power of projection which distinguishes normal from pathological motility. Their failure here once agains calls into question the psychologists' reliance on either positivistic induction and causal explanation, or on purely rationalistic analysis and reconstruction. Empiricist psychology typically tries to explain the behaviour of patients like Schneider by regarding it as a function of some deficiency in one or other of the senses. Schneider's difficulty in recognizing objects or performing abstract movements with his eyes closed, prompts the empiricists to assign primacy to visual representation and to attribute the motor disturbances to a loss of visual qualities. But what about those patients who, while knowing how to knock at a door, cannot perform the action on command if the door is out of their reach – even though they are looking directly at it? It would seem then that tactile perception rather than visual representation ought to be considered primary, and morbid motility explained by a loss of 'the sense of potential touch'. However, neither explanation is conclusive; it is just as plausible to maintain that the door must be within these patients' reach precisely because a deficiency in their sight renders vision inadequate to provide by itself the requisite background for action, thus making touch necessary as well. Which of the two – visual representation or tactile perception – is to be deemed the cause of abstract movement in normal persons? The question is unanswerable definitively within the

The power of projection = what Schneider lacks
↳ that which determines one's way of being in the world

empiricist framework, and it is totally misconceived from the viewpoint of existential analysis. As Merleau-Ponty notes, in the study of human behaviour 'it becomes clear that the facts are ambiguous, that no experiment is decisive and no explanation final'. Empiricism's approach is faulty in that it attempts to juxtapose the senses, focuses exclusively on their contents which it reduces to collections of sense data, and considers the pathology to be caused by a deficiency in one sense deemed primary. As a result, empiricism obscures the central phenomenon – namely, the power of projection – which is irreducible to any sense or inner sensibilities, although manifested in all. Existential analysis, drawing on the insights of Gestalt psychology, shows that content cannot be divorced from form and reduced to collections of sensible qualities. Moreover, the various senses cannot be isolated from each other and related to behaviour as variables to a function. Instead, they are mutually implicatory and inseparably integrated; as such, they establish a spatial organization. The normal subjects' way of structuring their environment differs from that of patients, and in both cases we are dealing with an experience which cannot be reduced to a summation of sensory contents. Consequently, as Merleau-Ponty says, 'psychological blindness, deficiency of sense of touch and motor disturbances are three *expressions* of a more fundamental disturbance through which they can be understood and not three component factors of morbid behaviour'. As we have seen, that fundamental disorder has to do with a power of projection which determines one's entire way of being-in-the-world.

Intellectualism, for its part, obscures this power of projection by focusing exclusively on form and seeking to establish 'a *reason* or intelligible condition of possibility' for the patient's various disturbances. In positing an entirely transparent consciousness, the intellectualists are forced to reduce error and illness to mere appearance. Such an intellectualist approach distorts even intellectual activity itself as it is found in the normal subject. Intellectualism considers thinking to be primarily a categorial operation; but 'living thought' in normal persons does not consist in performing purely logical operations. On the contrary, the need to engage explicitly in such operations is precisely what distinguishes impaired thought like that of Schneider from normal thinking. Healthy persons are object-orientated body-subjects who have an already acquired 'world of thoughts' at their disposal and can use this acquisition spontaneously in order to express something new in the course of a conversation, without needing to re-synthesize concepts and judgements continually. Unlike Schneider, normal persons do not perceive almost-amorphous patches to which they then laboriously assign significances through an act of the understanding. Rather, they discover a significance which permeates the object and they engage in an ongoing 'subject–object dialogue'. Schneider can arrive at intellectual significances by his painstaking analyses, but he lacks that 'primary [significance] reached through coexistence'. Hence, despite the fact that he possesses thoughts and words, he cannot use these freely to arrive at religious or political opinions; nor can he speak extemporaneously. He is totally caught up in the present, and cannot consider his past as a whole nor envisage his future as anything more than a 'shrunken' extension of the present. Thus it is the entire 'intentional arc' which has gone limp in Schneider.

This intentional arc is neither that reflex arc posited by mechanistic physiology nor that pure power of representation invoked by intellectualist psychology. It is anterior to the traditional distinctions, being inseparably vision, comprehension and motion. It is the living body which at this primordial level projects, apprehends and understands significances; and it does so in that fundamental dialectic between body-subject and world of which Merleau-Ponty spoke in the 'Preface'. At the dawn of perception in earliest infancy the living body, which is an anonymous synthesis of sensori-motor powers, outlines those 'indeterminate horizons' which signal the emergence of a world for us. As fundamental project our body has a temporal structure enabling it to carry this primitive acquisition of horizons along, so that a more determinate world of objects can begin to exist. The intellectualist analysis completely misses the being of this living body by insisting on an 'all or nothing' approach. If significance is entirely on the side of consciousness conceived as 'Mind', then the body can be no more than essentially meaningless matter. Disorders of the sort discussed above become incomprehensible since consciousness does not admit of degrees. Consciousness either categorizes data – in which case the person is healthy – or it ceases to exist altogether; patients become mechanistic objects. The intellectualist interpretation of human existence (as an activity of pure thought somehow informing a bodily mechanism) must therefore be rejected.

The rejection of empiricism on the one hand and intellectualism on the other, does not of course dictate an uncritical adherence to common sense. The world is not ready-made as common sense supposes it to be; rather it is 'built up', and the dialectical movement whereby it takes shape cannot be broken apart into so many self-contained fragments. The consideration of habits reveals this especially well. As Merleau-Ponty points out, to learn to type or play an instrument, to become accustomed to a vehicle or a cane or a feathered hat, 'is to be transplanted into them, or conversely, to incorporate them into the bulk of the body itself '.* Acquiring such habits is neither a matter of intellectual analysis and reconstruction nor a mechanical recording of impressions, as the adjustment to an unfamiliar car or keyboard makes evident. It is a question, rather, of the bodily comprehension of a motor significance which enables me to lend myself completely to expressing the music without having to think about the position of my fingers, or to manoeuvre my car successfully through a narrow street without having to compare the width of my vehicle with that of the driving lane. Merleau-Ponty's existential analysis of habits thus draws our attention to a new meaning of both 'knowledge' and 'meaning' which eludes the traditional approaches. The bodily knowledge and bodily significance which become evident in the study of habits reveal that 'the body is essentially an expressive space' in virtue of which particular expressive spaces (such as those of the piano which I have learned to play and the typewriter which I have mastered) can come into existence and be incorporated into it. Bodily spatiality, inherently dynamic, is the very condition for the coming into being of a meaningful world. Thus it subtends our entire existence as human beings.

---

* I have altered Colin Smith's translation in accordance with the French text.

4

The Synthesis of the Body Itself*

and

5

The Body in its Sexual Being

We have seen that the body as incarnate intentionality inhabits space and projects itself towards a perceptual world. In perception the various senses do not function as factors to be co-ordinated, but as indivisible powers structuring the world in a unified experience. Further, just as bodily spatiality is constitutive of the very being of the phenomenal body, so the spatiality of perceived things is inseparable from their being as things. Subject and world form an organically related whole, as the existential analysis of habit reveals so well. The consideration of our lived experience shows us that the body is not a mechanistic system consisting of parts externally related to one another in objective space. The body's parts do not impinge upon each other in a stimulus–response chain reaction; nor are they 'hooked up' into various patterns by the synthesizing activity of an intellect. While it is true that we can experience our body in this fashion, we have seen that such experience is abnormal, and that it is itself based on a primordial experience of the body as pre-objectively present to the world. At this pre-objective level, there is a fundamental dialectic,

---

* As in the previous chapter, I have translated 'le corps propre' as 'the body itself'.

48

a to-and-fro movement of an as-yet anonymous existence which *is* the living body and which comes into being as a body only in this very movement. Thus the living body is first of all an organic unity of sensibilities which already point beyond themselves in so far as they imply that which can be sensed and are already drawn towards it. Merleau-Ponty speaks of a 'force', 'momentum' or 'motivation' here. The body, as synthetic unity of sensory powers, solicits that which can be sensed and is itself attracted by the sensible as that in which these sensory powers are actualized. Bodily existence is thus already primordial transcendence towards something; and it implies both spatiality and temporality. As primitive project, bodily existence is precisely that movement which lays down spatio-temporal axes with reference to which particular sensibles are oriented. Bodily spatiality is not an acquired characteristic but rather, the very 'way in which the body comes into being as a body'.

Existence is never utterly blind; there is always already an amorphous pre-personal awareness of this primordial movement of the body towards the world. The body experiences itself to the extent that it perceives something else; and this anonymous self-reference is what makes possible the more explicit self-reference of specifically personal existence. The lived body is a system of equivalences. This means that its parts – or powers – are not externally but rather internally related through mutual implication. They do not mechanically trigger each other off, nor are they coordinated in some intellectual fashion. Each power is a power only in virtue of its position in the bodily schema; thus each power is already inherently related to all the others. The actualization of any one power implies any of a variety of ways in which the others can re-group themselves accordingly. The unity of the body involves an 'implicatory structure' in which powers can spontaneously compensate for – though not entirely replace – each other if the need arises. If my gaze is attracted by a vase on my desk, for example, the way in which my eyes move in examining it already indicates the manner in which my fingers can explore it; moreover, the former solicits the latter. If my fingers respond to this solicitation, the rest of my body spontaneously re-arranges itself around this new task – for example, my torso moves forward and my right arm straightens out as it reaches across the desk. Alternatively, if my arm is broken and in a plaster cast, my left arm can do the reaching; or I can stand up, walk around to the other side of my desk, reach down and pick the vase up. A description of such actions, or of habitual ones like picking up a pen to write, elucidates the general synthesis of the body.

Nevertheless, such a description in dealing with our customary world fails to illuminate that 'primary process of signification' whereby the world comes into being for us. Any description of the body's relationship to things in the world tends to present those things as already constituted, as existing in themselves independently of any bodily transcendence. Thus the relationship between bodily transcendence and the thing is all too easily reduced again to an epistemological problem – namely, that of determining how the human subject knows an already constituted object. Mind and body, subject and world, consequently fall apart into the traditional dualisms. We must therefore ask ourselves whether there is any area of our experience in which we can recapture that fundamental dialectic whereby something begins to exist for us, begins to have meaning for us to the extent that our body is a power of transcendence towards it. At this primitive level there is a primordial flow of existence in which something becomes significant to the extent that it attracts our body in a movement towards it, and our body comes into existence as a body in this very movement, so that the significance of the thing and that of the body come into existence together and imply one another. The body shows us this fundamental dialectic most adequately if we consider it in its sexual being.

It is a commonplace that a being who attracts us, who has for us a sexual significance, may not have such a significance for someone else. Consequently we are less tempted to consider the significance here as being already constituted, as belonging to that being in the manner in which hair belongs to the body. We will see here that the sexual significance of that being comes into existence for us and by us, rather than *ex nihilo*; but it does so only insofar as it is already outlined there in that being. The being who attracts us is a power of projection appealing to our *incarnate* subjectivity. In sexuality we are therefore best able to appreciate that significance is neither something given, or inert, in the manner of a traditional sense-datum, nor something simply conceived and imposed by a pure consciousness. Sexual significance is created in a living dialogue in which my body begins to exist for me in a new way in responding to another incarnate subjectivity. Any causal account of sexuality distorts the phenomenon. To the extent that a being *appeals* or beckons to me, that being cannot be utterly inert; and to the extent that I feel myself *drawn* towards that being, I cannot be a pure consciousness. The investigation of human sexuality will therefore bring to light the body as neither passivity nor activity but a third sort of being, by and for whom a third sort of significance comes to exist. We will then be in a better position to understand human relationships in general and, by extension, the life of society and the meaning of history as it ceaselessly comes into being by and for human beings. In focusing on the body in its sexual being we shall not lose what has already been gained up to this point – namely, the synthesis of the body, its implicatory structure. Quite the contrary will be the case, for in sexuality the 'gearing' of tactile, visual and motor powers into one another emerges more clearly than before.

As usual, Merleau-Ponty proceeds by an examination of the *breakdown* of the body's sexual being, in order that the normal body's sexual being might be thrown into relief for us. Our subject again is Schneider, whose troubles ultimately arise from an injury at the back of his head. If we adopt a mechanistic–physiological view of sexuality and conceive it as an autonomous reflex apparatus – a matter of the stimulation and response of a sex organ anatomically defined – it is difficult to account for the breakdown of sexuality in Schneider. Since his genitals are intact, it is hard to see why a head injury should inhibit sexual activity. As Merleau-Ponty notes, one would in fact expect the opposite – heightened sexual activity – to occur insofar as any intellectual constraints have become inoperative. On the other hand, if one adopts a more sophisticated mechanistic–physiological view, one might argue that sexuality is not a matter of an autonomous reflex apparatus, but rather involves a more complicated circuit going to the brain and having something to do with the back of the skull. However, on this account one would expect all forms of sexual activity to break down completely in Schneider. It thus becomes difficult to account for such phenomena as nocturnal emissions or to understand how Schneider can still take part in intercourse and even achieve orgasm, provided that his partner takes all the initiative. A purely physiological account could only explain either a heightening of sexual activity or a complete cessation of such activity. It is at a loss to account for a fundamental change in the very structure of erotic experience, such as we find in Schneider's case.

If we therefore adopt the intellectualist rather than the physiological view of human sexuality and emphasize the role of representations, we find ourselves no more capable of understanding

Schneider's condition. We may argue, for example, that sexuality is primarily a matter of associating psychological or emotional states like pleasure and pain, with certain ideas or representations, such that the latter can call up the former. An idea or mental image of an erotic object or situation would then bring into existence the erotic pleasure with which it has formerly been associated. However, apart from accounting for the phenomenon of association itself, this intellectualist approach runs into difficulty as soon as it tries to argue that what Schneider has lost is a certain collection of images or representations roughly labelled 'sexual'. The problem here is that we can present Schneider with what he has supposedly lost – we can show him obscene pictures or nude bodies; we can present him with erotic films; we can present him with 'sexual' ideas by talking to him about sexuality – but none of this has the power to arouse sexual desire in him. The fact is that Schneider for example still sees a nude woman and still feels the touch of her lips as she kisses him; but what he sees and feels no longer has the same meaning for him – it lacks a sexual significance. The female body no longer attracts him; he no longer apprehends it as an appeal. This happens precisely to the extent that Schneider's own bodily being has ceased to be an active transcendence. For Schneider, female bodies are indistinguishable physically; and to the extent that he considers a woman attractive, it is merely a matter of her character. This indicates to us that normal human sexuality involves a physical aura which makes it irreducible to an intellectual significance. For healthy persons, all bodies do *not* have the same significance, despite the fact that they all have roughly the same physiological features. Sexual significance must therefore be inseparable from, but irreducible to, the physicality of the human body. For normal persons, that body is subtended by a strictly individual 'sexual schema'. In so far as sexual significance is not a given datum for a disembodied consciousness, its apprehension requires that we not rest in the actual, in the already constituted realm of things, but that we actively project ourselves – in our bodily being – beyond the given in order to endow it with significance. As we have seen, Schneider has lost this ability to use his body freely to project around himself a situation into which he can throw himself. Since he 'can no longer put himself into a sexual situation', he cannot apprehend such a situation either, because transcendence and apprehension are inseparable moments of a fundamental dialectic.

We are now in a position to understand what Merleau-Ponty means when he says that the body is comparable to a work of art because expression and what is expressed are indistinguishable in both cases. The sexual significance of the body *is* a certain style of bodily existence and is irreducible to any intellectual conception. In an analogous fashion, significance pervades a painting or musical composition and comes into being for us if we use our eyes or ears respectively in such a way that the colours or notes assume their unique style. Similarly, the sexual significance of another body comes into being for us only insofar as we use our sensibilities in such a way that that body's features assume for us a certain sexual style. The apprehension of sexual significance thus requires an active transcendence in which the various sensibilities of the body-subject participate; hence it might be objected that Merleau-Ponty's account makes sexual significance synonymous with existential significance in general, and absorbs sexuality into existence. Yet as Merleau-Ponty himself notes, impaired sexuality does not rule out an effective political life for example, nor does technical virtuosity in sex necessarily imply any particular perfection or vigour in other areas of one's life. Sexuality is not reducible to existence, nor existence reducible to sexuality. Existence is a more general current which structures itself in various ways, and 'the sexual life is a sector of our life bearing a special relation to the existence of sex'. As we have seen, there can be no question of reducing sexuality to the genital or relegating it to a psyche understood as pure consciousness or spirit. Indeed, Merleau-Ponty's phenomenological description of the body has shown us the need to replace such conceptions as the 'purely bodily' and 'purely psychic' with the notion of an incarnate subjectivity in whom all sectors of experience 'interfuse' in such a way that each remains distinctive while none is entirely isolable. The traditional notion of the unconscious has no place here; incarnate existence is not a matter of 'distinct representations' supported and explained by 'unconscious representations'. The body is the expression of existence, but this does not mean that the former is a mere accompaniment to the latter, or that either is 'the original of the human being'. Each presupposes the other in that primary process whereby meaning comes into being and an original style emerges.

As a form of this primary process, sexuality is a particular dialectic expressing existence. Merleau-Ponty bases himself on Sartre's discussion of being-for-others in *Being and Nothingness* to draw our attention to the nature of this dialectic and its metaphysical significance. In the experience of shame as Sartre shows, we are uncomfortably aware that another person has reduced us to the status of an object by his look. The fact that we have a body makes such objectification an ever present possibility on the one hand and, on the other, enables us to break free and reassert our subjectivity by submitting the other person to a similarly alienating gaze. But as Hegel noted, this master–slave dialectic is inherently self-subverting in so far as only another subject can accord us the kind of recognition we seek. Sexual desire displays the same dialectic to the extent that we use our body to fascinate the other, only to discover that what we desire eludes us. We want to possess 'not just a body, but a body brought to life by consciousness'; yet the effort to gain possession strips the other of that very consciousness in reducing him to the status of a thing to be grasped. Sexual life thus brings to light the fundamental ambiguity of the human body and expresses those aspects of freedom and dependence which characterize human existence in general. Existence can absorb itself to a greater or lesser degree in the body, as shown by Merleau-Ponty's example of the patient who lost her voice when forbidden to see her lover, or as shown in attempts to make oneself into a fascinating object in order to entice and ensnare the other's freedom. However, the body can never shut itself off from the world altogether, or become completely reduced to an object. As a synthesis of powers the body is always already to some extent a transcendence, a project in which existence, body and world are inseparable. The body is a body instead of a corpse only because existence animates it and conversely, existence must incarnate itself and in so doing it already brings about an incarnate meaning.

Incarnate existence is characterized by an inherent ambiguity, a basic indeterminacy, because it is a continually composed synthesis of powers, 'a nexus of living [significances]'. The bodily project always involves the coming into being of meanings which cannot be separated out because they are mutually implicatory and already point beyond themselves. The ambiguity and indeterminacy of incarnate existence is especially evident in sexuality where, as we have seen, an inherent instability characterizes our experience of the body as both a subject for us and an object for someone else. Sexual significance manifests itself in the whole manner of the body-subject – in the bearing, the gestures, the movements, the voice – and the interfusion of visual, motor, auditory, and tactile aspects is singularly evident in its coming into being. Yet for the most part, that significance is not clear-cut but rather exists as 'an ambiguous atmosphere' which lends itself to a variety of significances in that dynamic co-existence which is the very fabric of human life. As we have seen, the apprehension of a sexual significance presupposes the ability to put ourselves into a situation; this fundamental power simultaneously enables us to take up and transform a *de facto* situation, so that 'what had only a sexual meaning assumes a more general significance'.* However, as transcendence, incarnate existence never outstrips that which it transcends; neither is it ever reducible to that which is transcended. In either case, transcendence would cease to be transcendence – but since existence *is* transcendence, this would in fact spell death. It is in this sense that Merleau-Ponty contends that 'no one is saved and no one is totally lost'.

Because we are body-subjects, we can neither leave behind our bodily being nor discard our subjectivity. Furthermore, bodily being is not a purely factual physicality, and subjectivity is not a purely translucent consciousness. We are not an uneasy alliance of matter and mind, but a third kind of being. Salvation would mean a definitive escape from ambiguity; yet in so far as our existence is dialectical, ambiguity is of its essence. Damnation, on the other hand, would involve the permanent sealing of our existence into one definitive significance. This too is ruled out in so far as openness is part and parcel of transcendence; as movement *beyond*, transcendence is incompatible with reduction to any given X. It is always an act involving relation and incorporation – thus a continual transformation of the given. In short, the apprehension of any significance whatsoever presupposes existence as transcendence, and transcendence always already transforms everything with which it is presented – precisely because it takes it up and assigns it a place in the general dialectic of existence. Moreover, as the phenomenological account of the body in its sexual being has shown, transcendence is not a solitary project. Human existence is essentially co-existence; there is a web of interacting transcendences eliciting, apprehending and carrying forward multi-faceted meanings in all dimensions. Now that we have considered sexuality as an expression of existence, we must examine expression itself more closely.

---

* I have altered Colin Smith's translation to bring it into line with the original text.

6
The Body as Expression and Speech

If we examine our pre-reflective lived experience, so Merleau-Ponty has argued, we realize that our body is not a system of externally related parts but rather, that it displays a spontaneous synthesis of powers, a bodily spatiality, a bodily unity, a bodily intentionality, which distinguish it radically from the scientific object posited by traditional schools of thought. In the last chapter Merleau-Ponty described how the apprehension of sexual significance reveals a pre-reflective bodily intentionality such that something begins to exist for us precisely to the extent that the body is a power of transcendence towards it. One might still contend, nonetheless, that this talk of a *bodily* intentionality is really no more than a metaphor based on a *genuine* intentionality which is to be found exclusively in the realm of thought. One would insist that after all we should turn our attention to the fact that *we* are *thinking* about our lived experience. We will see then, so one might argue, that there is a realm of subjectivity quite distinct from that of our bodily experience, and that this realm of thought, or consciousness, or reflection is the realm of significance and intentionality in their *proper* sense. The domain of subjectivity will thus be declared to be quite distinct from that other realm of the body, or objectivity. We thereby return to the traditional idea of an 'inner life' contingently linked to the body – in short, to the old mind–body or subject–object dualism. Merleau-Ponty must therefore show that the realm of thought is 'of a piece' with the pre-reflective experience of the body. Otherwise, his phenomenological descriptions up to this point might be taken to indicate merely that there is no body-world dichotomy, but *not* that the traditional distinction between mind and body is inappropriate. The body would then take up its traditional position among things in the world and thought would once more become the proper realm of philosophical investigation. To rule this out, Merleau-

Ponty must be able to point to an internal, or essential, relation-ship between thought and the body.

It is usually conceded that there is such an essential relationship between hearing and the eardrums, or between speaking and the vocal chords, and that the brain likewise plays a crucial part in such communication. Most of us thus have no difficulty in granting that hearing and speaking have to do with the body. The problem comes when we consider the relationship between thought and the body, because we usually assume the existence of an 'inner life', or realm of pure thought, and consider the connec-tion of this with what is spoken or heard to be one of translation or interpretation. In short, most of us tend to think that to speak is to translate our thoughts into words, while to hear is to interpret the words of another so as to arrive at an understanding of the thoughts lying behind them. We allegedly attempt to 'figure out' what others 'have in mind' by inference based on the words which we hear them say. It is evident that this sort of position rests on a fundamental mind-body dualism. It thus calls for a re-examination; and since speaking and hearing incontestably in-volve language, it is language itself which Merleau-Ponty must reconsider in the present chapter.

The inadequacy of traditional approaches once again emerges most clearly through the study of pathological cases. Psychologists initially argued that amnesia involved the loss of physical or psychic 'traces' of words imprinted on the brain or psyche in the course of linguistic experience. Possessing such 'verbal images' constituted possessing language; and articulation was produced automatically by a purely physical stimulus–response circuit which revived the verbal image, or through acquired mental associations. Both views reduced speech to a third person pheno-menon consisting of a stream of words which were themselves bereft of meaning or power. Such mechanistic theories failed to account for the fact that patients who readily produced the requisite words in the context of 'concrete language', failed to find those same words in 'gratuitous language' when confronted with exercises lacking emotional or vital import. Most cases of aphasia proved to be inexplicable in terms of the loss of verbal images; rather, the decisive factor seemed to be the function of the words – whether they served as instruments of action or were called upon simply for disinterested specification. Psychologists further dis-covered that patients who could not produce the names of colours with which they were confronted, likewise were unable to classify the colours when requested to sort samples. The problem thus seemed to lie in a disorder of thinking which restricted these patients to 'the concrete attitude' – making it virtually impossible for them to transcend the individual sensory given, so as to recognize it as subsumable under a category and to name it accordingly. This disturbance of thought could not itself be explained as resulting from a loss of verbal images; therefore it seemed that language must depend upon thought; accordingly, psychologists constructed intellectualist theories of language and sought to explain the divers cases of aphasia as resulting from a breakdown of the categorial operation. Words became merely the external trappings of an internal thinking; once again, the words themselves had no meaning or power. Language was simply a contingent container into which the thinking subject poured thought and it was thought which had the meaning. Everything rested on the categorial activity of thinking; articulation remained an involuntary action – the product of a physiological or psychic mechanism. In the intellectualists' view, as in the case of the empiricist psychologies, there was no *speaking* subject. Language was now only the accompaniment of a purely cognitive operation which it presupposed and which was essentially self-sufficient. However, whereas empiricism had been perplexed by patients' inability to find in gratuitous language words available to them in concrete situations, intellectualism was bewildered by cases in which patients were unable to categorize colour samples while nonetheless able to name the colours.

Merleau-Ponty goes beyond the empiricist and the intellectualist theories by declaring that '*the word has a meaning*'; in place of the traditional positions, he outlines a phenomenological approach and develops what he calls 'an existentialist theory of aphasia'. Despite its appearance to the contrary, intellectualism was no more satisfactory than was empiricism in accounting for various forms of aphasia; moreover, neither approach provided a theory of language which was true to our actual experience. Merleau-Ponty points out that thought does not itself suffice for recognizing things; nor does speech presuppose thinking. In fact, there can be no pure thought prior to speech. Lacking all supports, such thought would vanish instantly and we could never be aware of it. Our experience shows us that even familiar objects appear indeterminate until we remember their names; consequently, naming *is* recognition. In our actual denomination of objects, we do not have in mind a concept under which we would subsume them; instead, the names themselves bear the meaning and we are aware of reaching the objects in imposing their names. We ourselves do not know our own thoughts until we formulate them in 'internal or external speech'; hence, it is evident that speaking accomplishes thought rather than merely translating an already accomplished thought.

Authentic speech *is* the presence of thought in the world – not its garment, but its body. Communication with others would be impossible if authentic expression were not identical with thinking; unless the listener can learn something from the speaker's words themselves, communication becomes an illusion. Yet our own experience belies the view that others' words are merely mechanisms for arousing thoughts which we ourselves possess all along. It is true, of course, that communication presupposes a shared language; but such a language must itself have come into existence at some time – it is not a natural endowment. If we are to avoid an infinite regress – which would make the actual existence of a common language incomprehensible – we must acknowledge that originating speech possesses an immanent *'gestural [signifi-cance]'*. To bring this significance to light, Merleau-Ponty draws our attention to the experience of saying and thinking, or hearing, something new. The speaker does not precede or accompany his speech by thought; he neither visualizes his words nor concep-tualizes their meaning. He simply uses a common language in such a way that a new significance comes into being as he speaks. His speech is not a sign of some internal operation; rather, it *is* his thought. Likewise, the listener neither decodes signs nor concep-tualizes what he hears; he understands the other's new signifi-cance as it emerges and unfolds. There is no thinking paralleling or following his listening; his listening is his thinking. Speaker and listener are subjects inhabiting a shared linguistic world; and just as they have no need to visualize either their limbs or external space in moving around in the natural world, so they have no need in communication to visualize the words located in their linguistic world. In both cases they are situated in a world and their activity realizes a potential use of their body. The consideration of authentic speech thus alerts us to the existential significance which underlies the conceptual significance of language.

This existential significance permeates the words themselves and is imparted by them, just as the musical significance of a concerto inhabits the sounds which bring that significance into

being for the concert goer. Despite the fact that speech is uniquely
capable of constituting 'an acquisition for use in human relationships', it is just as erroneous to regard thought as divorceable from
its expression in speech, as to regard music as detachable from its
expression in sounds. Speech is no more an envelope or 'outer
covering' of thought than are the notes of the music or the marks
made by the brush on the canvas merely external accessories of the
concerto or the landscape painting respectively. In speech, as in
music or painting, it is successful expression which brings a new
significance into being and opens up new possibilities for our
experience. Our usual tendency to regard speech as incidental to
an autonomous thought, arises from our failure to distinguish
adequately between originating speech and 'second order' language. That which we commonly consider silence or 'pure thought'
is in fact replete with words. The so-called 'silent inner life' is
actually a monologue in which we formulate our thoughts by
employing the already constituted significances created by former
acts of expression – whether our own or those of others. Unlike
first order expression, our everyday speech remains within the
circuit of acquired significances; it does not elicit any new
thoughts, but merely reinforces the already existing ones. Second
order speech thus conceals from us the phenomenon of authentic
expression by giving us the illusion that we possess thoughts
which do not depend on any words whatsoever.

If we are to appreciate the nature of originating speech, we must
go beyond the realm of constituted speech and become aware of
that inchoate primordial silence from which the latter once arose.
Merleau-Ponty insists that the 'spoken word is a genuine gesture,
and [that] it contains its meaning in the same way as the gesture
contains its'. Modern psychologists have shown that contrary to
what had been thought, the understanding of gestures does not in
fact require any introspection. Moreover, such introspection
would fail to furnish an association between the alleged inner
states and their outward manifestations, because the latter elude
the actor. Besides, our experience reveals that we do not apprehend gestures as signs of psychic facts. For example, gestures do
not for the viewer represent concealed emotions; they *are* those
emotions. The fist shaken under my nose does not prompt me to
think of anger; it *is* the anger and I immediately apprehend it as
such. This is not to say, however, that we perceive the meaning of
gestures as we perceive colour qualities, since we fail to under-

stand the gestures of animals or even of people belonging to a very different culture. The meaning of gestures is understood, rather than being given like a physical phenomenon. Communication and comprehension of a gesture are achieved through the establishing of a reciprocity between the other's intention and my own. Neither his intention nor mine is thematized; in both cases it 'inhabits' our body. Our interaction involves neither a mechanical process nor an intellectual operation, but a pre-reflective act of structuring the world on the part of one body-subject and a corresponding pre-reflective act of recapturing the meaning of that structuration on the part of the other incarnate subject. What we have here is a pre-reflective dialogue involving an invitation to concur with a certain way of perceiving the world, and a response to that invitation by an adjusting of the body's powers so as to overlap the intentional object outlined by the other's gesture. In the case of originating speech, the listener's comprehension thus involves a modulation of his own being in response to the speaker's 'sense-giving intention' ['l'intention significative']. Neither one knows just where the speech will lead, since what is being created and communicated is precisely not a ready-made content. The speaker feels the need to speak without knowing exactly what he will say, and the listener takes up this intention by adjusting his own being to the speaker's style of being-in-the-world. Expression and comprehension are achieved through the body first and foremost; any intellectual clarification comes later. Communication thus understood is no more mysterious than is the perception of objects, for in both cases we experience a 'bodily presence' which is prior to any scientific conception of the event.

Merleau-Ponty acknowledges that, given the plethora of existing languages, the connection between the word and its significance seems purely arbitrary. Traditionally, speech has therefore been distinguished from gesture by designating the former 'a conventional sign' and the latter 'a natural sign'. However, if we go beyond the conceptual to the emotional – or gestural – meaning of words, we discover that they too possess an immanent significance. In poetry we see most readily that the words themselves express the emotional essence of that which they designate. Different languages express different ways of being-in-the-world; hence the nuances – 'the *full meaning*' – of one cannot be rendered by another, as translators know only too well. The meaning is inseparable from the particular language; this is not, however, to adopt the opposite extreme of the traditional conception of language by declaring it to be a system of natural signs instead of mere convention. In fact, it is neither for the simple reason that both conceptions miss the essence of the human world. The dawn of language lies in emotional gesticulation; but the latter – contrary to popular belief – is itself not 'natural' in the sense of being given with the structure of the human body itself. As Merleau-Ponty points out, a comparison of a Japanese with an Occidental shows that 'it is no more natural, and no less conventional, to shout in anger or to kiss in love than to call a table "a table" '. Neither thought nor emotion is divorceable from the body; yet both are irreducible to its anatomical makeup. There is no transparent, self-subsistent thought translatable into divers languages; nor is there a pure emotion disclosable by identical or different gestures. Thought and emotion are modes of being-in-the-world, and the differences between the language and gestures of one people and those of another testify to their different ways of perceiving stimuli and responding to situations. Thus 'the difference of behaviour corresponds to a difference in the emotions themselves', although any attempt to separate the one from the other is fundamentally wrongheaded. The biological body does not come equipped with a ready-made, immutable human nature; there is no 'natural' behaviour subtending cultural 'conventions'. A fundamental ambiguity distinguishes human life from animal life, such that everything in the former is simultaneously 'natural' and 'cultural' – nothing is absolutely independent of 'purely biological being', yet everything transcends it. Like the significance of other forms of behaviour, the significance of speech is both immanent and transcendent – it is immanent in the behaviour itself, but irreducible to the anatomical apparatus as such. Like everything else, speech is a way of living one's body in the world, and it too involves a simultaneous modulation of both. Our usual conceptions of necessity and contingency are inadequate to capture the being of verbal gesticulation, just as they are inappropriate for comprehending the character of sexual being. In both cases, it is a question of appropriating and transforming a given situation by a kind of 'escape' which ensures our freedom – while precluding its ever being absolute. Nothing in human existence is utterly fortuitous or totally conditioned, and despite their appearance to the contrary, neither linguistic nor other gestures constitute exceptions.

The phenomenological approach thus reveals speech to be a particular form of that fundamental project which the previous chapters have already shown to define our very existence as human beings in the world. This primordial power of transcendence involves the apprehending of the creating and communicating of a meaning which comes from nowhere and is irreducible to anything else. The primacy of the linguistic meaning has to do with its ability to become sedimented into an intersubjective acquisition for future use in the quest for truth – a never-ending quest whose origin lies in speech itself. The open-ended nature of experience which the very notion of transcendence already implies, is perhaps nowhere more evident than in linguistic expression – and disorders affecting such expression most readily bring it to our attention. The modern theory of aphasia, developed by such psychologists as Grünbaum and Goldstein, confirms this phenomenological conception of language and overcomes the problems encountered by the empiricist and intellectualist accounts. According to Merleau-Ponty, these modern psychologists are in fact attempting to formulate what he calls 'an existential theory of aphasia' in which external language and thought are considered manifestations of the fundamental project described above. In aphasia these phenomena lose their existential significance for the patient, thereby indicating a breakdown in the basic activity of transcendence itself. Earlier we saw that patients suffering from amnesia regarding colour names are likewise unable to classify colour samples. Intellectualism considered the disturbance in categorial activity to signal a disorder of thought, which it deemed primary. The existential theory of aphasia goes beyond this sort of explanation by basing itself on the modern psychologists' concrete descriptions of such cases. The latter reveal that the disorder has to do with the very way in which the patients relate themselves to the world and accordingly, with the style or shape of their experience itself. This prompts us to recognize that the categorial activity is not simply or primarily a matter of thinking or judging. Prior to its being a thought or a form of cognition, it is a way of situating oneself in the world and concomitantly, structuring one's experience. Whereas the normal subjects' perception organizes itself into figure–background structures in keeping with the required task, the patients' perception remains essentially passive – with the result that each item stays shut up in its own individual being. Consequently, for the latter objectively similar colour samples need not appear to be similar at all; the patients' gaze might be arrested by the degree of warmth in one sample and by the basic shade in another. The patients' entire attitude towards the world differs from that of normal subjects; unlike the latter, the former fail to detect any intention in the perceptible world.

As we have seen, the loss of this power to apprehend an existential significance corresponds to a breakdown, in the patients' power to create and communicate such significance. The basic intentionality of the body itself has bogged down; and the disturbances of speech and thought are not an ultimate fact but rather, are themselves rooted in this principal inertia. The psychologists' studies disclose that many patients who are unable to classify colours are nevertheless able to repeat the colour names and associate ideas. It therefore becomes evident that their difficulty in categorizing colours is not due to a loss of words or extrinsic connections of meaning but rather, that it has to do with a loss of that living meaning which normally inhabits words. Thus the real link between language and thought becomes severed, leaving patients with colour names which no longer signify anything for them. By contrast, normal subjects' categorial behaviour and use of words point to a radically different manner of being-in-the-world. Unlike the psychologists' patients, they experience a bodily intentionality which opens them to the perceptible world, enabling them to discern its significance and to structure it according to present demands. This pre-reflective incarnate intentionality further allows normal subjects to project themselves towards a world of 'the mind' or the imagination, and to participate actively in cultural life. Language is inseparable here from this basic activity of transcendence, so that their language *is* their 'taking up of a position' in this 'mental' or cultural world. Merleau-Ponty stresses that just as for normal subjects a pattern of their bodily behaviour invests the surrounding objects with a particular significance for themselves and others, so their 'phonetic "gesticulation" ' – their speech – brings about a certain intersubjective co-ordinating of experience. The analysis of aphasia and the normal experience which it brings to light by contrast, make it clear that speech is not reducible to either motility or intelligence. Instead it is both simultaneously, and is itself part of that fundamental power whereby normal human beings transcend a *de facto* situation and project themselves towards other people.

As we have seen, linguistic disorders take a whole variety of forms, sometimes affecting only a particular aspect of linguistic experience (the visual or the conceptual or the verbal) but sometimes altering the structure of experience in its entirety. Yet no matter how specific or how general the disturbance, it always touches the meaning of language and involves some sort of congealing of existence, thus impairing or destroying the normal openness of experience. In Schneider's case this congelation manifests itself in all areas: he cannot throw himself into an imaginary or creative situation, he cannot initiate sexual activity, he cannot use language to describe a merely possible experience, he cannot become involved in discussions on religious or political topics, he cannot speak unless he has prepared his speech, and he never experiences any need to speak. In short, he is incapable of an act of authentic expression – he cannot create any opening in being because his own experience totally lacks openness; for him, it is characterized by 'self-evidence and self-sufficiency'.

The striking contrast between the closed character of Schneider's experience and the essential openness of normal experience, parallels the radical difference between the traditional Cartesian conception of the body and soul on the one hand, and the phenomenological notion of incarnate subjectivity on the other. Indirectly drawing to our attention the enigmatic nature of the body itself, the consideration of speech and expression has definitively undermined the old view of the body as an agglomeration of self-enclosed particles or a network of third person processes. Speech and mute gestures have admittedly always been recognized as transfiguring the body; yet such transfigurations were deemed to be a disclosing of the thought or soul, which was itself considered to be essentially incorporeal. Though so to speak shining through the body and illuminating it, mind or soul was not *of* the body and was at best a temporary resident within it. As Merleau-Ponty points out however, speech or gesture could never express thought unless the body itself *were* that thought rather than its merely external indicator. In the absence of any immanent meaning, the body would be utterly incapable of projecting and communicating meaning. The Cartesian tradition has taught us to juxtapose thought and body, and to purge them of all ambiguity. We have thus long persuaded ourselves that we are composed of a transparent consciousness and a mechanistic object, both being entirely clear and self-enclosed yet somehow extrinsically linked together. Nevertheless, we have seen that even Descartes himself was ultimately at a loss as to how to conceive the union of mind and body thus defined; moreover, he clearly recognized the tremendous disparity between his own dualistic thesis and his actual experience of the body. Religious belief prompted Descartes to ascribe primacy to the former rather than the latter, and to rest his case on a non-deceiving God. For Merleau-Ponty, such an uncritical approach is quite unacceptable. Instead, he urges us to bring our conception of thought and the body into line with our pre-reflective experience. If we take seriously the phenomenological rediscovery of the body itself, we will be forced to recognize a third kind of existence which the Cartesian analysis systematically excludes. As soon as we relinquish our stubborn adherence to the Cartesian idea of the body and reconsider the lived body itself, we are compelled to acknowledge 'an ambiguous mode of existing' which overturns the traditional subject-object or mind-body categories. We must then discard the idea of causal connections among bodily functions on the one hand, and between the body and the 'external world' on the other. In place of such connections, we will be prompted to recognize fundamental relations of mutual implication having their roots in that central phenomenon of incarnate signification which the phenomenological description has brought to light. Mind or thought and body are themselves abstract moments of this central phenomenon. In abandoning the traditional procedure of detaching mind from body and subject from object, we reinstate the embodied subject as one who is 'never hermetically sealed' but rather, always already intentionally related to the world in some measure. Consequently, the rediscovery of incarnate subjectivity will lead us to revise as well our conception of the sensible world as a whole.

Part II
The Perceived World

The Theory of the Body
Is Already a Theory
of Perception

Merleau-Ponty's phenomenological description of the body has shown us the need to break with the entrenched dogmatisms and to recognize the body itself as inherently expressive of existence as a whole. We have traditionally tended to adopt either of two approaches: we have detached subjectivity from the body and made of the latter an object existing in-itself and reducible to the sum of its parts; or we have put the primacy on a thought which strips the body of its perspectivity and, in an allegedly clear and distinct idea, offers it up as an absolute object to the disinterested gaze of a disembodied consciousness. In either case, we have bypassed our actual experience and have chosen to ignore the fact that *the body is ourself*. By the same token, we have reflectively ejected ourselves from the perceived world and considered the latter a collection of self-enclosed objects existing independently of any perceiver; or we have purged the perceived world of its appearance and allegedly captured its reality in the clear and distinct ideas of an incorporeal, non-perspectival subject. Both views fundamentally distort our actual experience of being-in-the-world; but instead of renouncing these theories, we have for the most part chosen to discredit our experience. However, the difficulties which arose in attempting to account for various disorders have prompted us to question this traditional disparagement of experience and to revise our traditional conceptions. We have been led, for example, to transform the notion of body image so as to accommodate the findings of the psychologists, thereby relinquishing the idea of the body as mechanistic object and recognizing a bodily intentionality whose pole is the perceived world. We have thus reinstated the essential link between our body and the world; further, our study of sexuality, expression and speech has induced us to restore subjectivity to the body itself. Since the perceived world has emerged as a pole of bodily experience, and since the subject has recovered its body, the vital connection between body-subject and world has already implicitly been re-established. As the title of this introductory section indicates, 'the theory of the body is already a theory of perception'; consequently, we will need to revise explicitly our view of the perceived world so as to bring it into line with our amended conception of the body itself. Neither body nor world are extrinsic to the perceiver; rather, these terms are mutually implicatory. The unity of the perceptual world and the identity of any particular object seen from different perspectives successively, depend on the pre-reflective awareness of our motility as perceivers, and of our bodily identity through that motility. The very notion of objects having a position and an identity presupposes our bodily experience. Moreover, the latter is not a poor approximation of a comprehensive intellectual grasp of the object – on the contrary, such an all-encompassing grasp is an extravagant pretension predicated on that very experience itself. Prior to any intellectual conception of it, we experience the unity of the object as correlated to that of our body; and we experience our being *in* the world before we ever arrive at the idea of an *external* world.

Although it might seem that we destroy the objectivity of the object by reintegrating it into our bodily experience, this is in fact not so. It is true that we never experience all sides of a cube as equal – but this does not mean that the 'real' cube eludes our experience and that the latter must be interpreted in order that an intellectual reconstruction might render us the cube as it really is. Nor is the cube's meaning to be arrived at by a purely intellectual consideration. Any attempt to detach the object from the conditions under which we actually perceive it, is fatally flawed; the so-called 'real' cube consisting of six simultaneous and equal sides would be utterly inconceivable in the absence of our perceptual experience as embodied subjects. Underlying that reflective procedure which tears the subject away from its body and its world, we find a pre-reflective experience in which our body, things and the world are immediately present and interrelated in a 'living connection', just as are the parts of our body itself. Our conception of the thing and of the world ultimately rests on their perceptual self-evidence, and the latter is in turn inseparable from our pre-reflective awareness of the body itself. The pre-reflective synthesis of the body itself brings about the synthesis of the perceived object prior to any reflective reconstruction; moreover, these two syntheses are not two separate acts, but rather two aspects of a single act of perception. The structure of the phenomenal body already implies the structure of the entire perceptual field. It remains for us to suspend our traditional detached knowledge of the thing and the world in order that we may become aware of our actual perceptual experience.

1

Sensing*

Empiricism and intellectualism presuppose a ready-made world in their analyses; consequently, both are oblivious to the subject of perception. The empiricist regards perception as merely one event among others occurring in the world, its locus being the perceiver. In studying the sensations which make up this occurrence, the empiricist adopts an impersonal approach – thereby totally neglecting the fact that he *lives* perception and *is* the perceiving subject even in his very study of perception itself. This detached approach which relegates perception to the status of a fact in an objective world, fails to recognize that perception is on the contrary the condition of there being any facts for us at all. The empiricist analysis belies that upon which it itself rests – namely, the lived transcendence which creates an opening in being and thereby brings about the presence of a perceptual field. Whereas the empiricist overlooks his own role in his analysis of perception, the intellectualist accords himself a role which makes his lived perception equally incomprehensible while depending upon it just as surely. The empiricist leaves no room for consciousness; the intellectualist subordinates everything to a universal constituting ego. The second position merely reverses the first in replacing being-in-itself by being-for-itself. The transcendental ego is not itself *involved* in perception; in constituting the world it remains beyond that world rather than within it, and establishes causal connections among the world, the body, and the empirical self. Since these are spread out before the thinker, the intellectualist cannot account for their never actually being perfectly explicit or complete for us. Like empiricism, intellectualism misses the perceiving subject and rules out perception as we actually live it. Inducive psychology can help us to reinstate the latter by challeng-

---

* Like Guerrière, I have decided to translate 'le Sentir' as 'Sensing', rather than as 'Sense Experience'. (See *Journal of the British Society for Phenomenology*, vol. 10, no. 1 (Jan. 1979) p. 67.)

ing both the empiricist and the intellectualist views of sensation as, respectively, a state or quality, and the consciousness of such a state or quality.

As we might expect, the true nature of sensation emerges most clearly through the study of experiments involving patients suffering from disorders – in this case, 'diseases of the cerebellum or the frontal cortex'. Psychologists discovered that alterations in the colour of the visual field brought about corresponding changes in the amplitude, direction, and accuracy of the patients' arm movements. The outward sweep or inward bend, the smoothness, the speed and so on, varied according to the colour – each colour always giving rise to the same tendency. One might be tempted to invoke a causal explanation, reducing the motor reaction to an effect mechanically produced by a physical phenomenon impinging on the objective body. However, such an explanation is precluded by the fact that colours which were created by contrast, possessed the same motor value as their actual colour counterparts. Yet this does not authorize us to adopt the opposite approach and decare that consciousness constitutes the colour's motor physiognomy out of some sort of mental stuff, or 'hylē'. In the latter case, the influence of colour on behaviour becomes inexplicable, as does the finding that the subject may be quite unaware of such influence even while reacting to it. A constituting consciousness would by definition be aware of what it was constituting and would presumably counteract any potential effect on behaviour; thus the constituting activity of consciousness not only renders the actual findings inexplicable, but is itself incomprehensible. We must cease to consider colour a purely physical phenomenon or an intellectual construction; instead, we must recognize sensation as a living dialogue between the body-subject and its existential environment.

Colour prompts the pre-reflective adoption of 'a certain bodily attitude'; the amplification or contraction of movements is part of that attitude and indicative of the particular hue. The terms of this dialogue are neither mutually external nor reducible to one another. Colour *is* a certain manner of being-in-the-world which implies the actual presence of a particular atmosphere and the body-subject's power of responding to it. Consequently, the presentation of a colour does not mechanically trigger off the adopting of the corresponding bodily disposition; nor does the taking up of a particular bodily attitude suffice for seeing the colour if the environment fails to offer the solicitation. Sensing is not an inexpressible coinciding with a sensible or an invasion by the latter; nor is it a purely subjective creating of an appearance or an intellectual positing of a meaning. The bodily intentionality which we have already encountered in previous chapters manifests itself here: it is not a disembodied observer but rather, a body-subject who sees and hears and touches the sensible. Sensing is neither a passive registering nor an active imposing of a meaning; to sense something is to co-exist or 'commune' with it, to open oneself to it and make it one's own prior to any reflection or specifically personal act. If we insist on regarding the world as pure matter and the subject as transparent consciousness, the phenomenological description of sensation as a form of co-existence, or communion between a body-subject and a being located beyond it, will seem confused at best. But as we have seen, it is the traditional dichotomy between being-in-itself and being-for-itself which, given the findings of psychology and our own experience, is itself unintelligible. If we suspend our philosophical prejudices, we will acknowledge readily enough that there is no thinker standing behind our ears or hands when we hear or touch something, or when we stretch out on the grass or the sand and lose ourselves in the azure sky overhead. Who among us has not had the experience of becoming one with the sky or the sea on a clear summer's day? Why should we dismiss that experience as a confusion or an illusion?

The subject of sensation is not that personal self which has opinions and makes decisions; rather, it is the pre-personal living body whose sense-powers are themselves so many 'natural selves'. By virtue of having a body, we are already in possession of sensory fields – that is, we open onto a sensible world within whose horizons all particular sensory givens are located, lending themselves to unending exploration. Sensing is thus an anonymous open-ended activity anterior to, and presupposed by, specifically personal existence. We commonly distinguish among the different senses, relegating vision to the eyes, audition to the ears, olfaction to the nose, taste to the taste buds of the tongue, and touch primarily to the hands. Indeed, Merleau-Ponty himself asserts that 'the self which sees or the self which hears is in some way a specialized self '. Do the various senses nonetheless communicate, and is there a unity of the senses? As we have seen, intellectualism subordinates everything to a constituting consciousness; in doing so, it effectively transcends the plurality of the senses. Although it distinguishes contingent matter from necessary form in analyzing knowledge, intellectualism considers matter to be inseparable from form in the actual act of knowing. On this view, knowledge is always knowledge of objects – broadly speaking – and space is 'the form of objectivity'. Consequently, the senses are all spatial since they provide access to objects; moreover, each sense opens onto the same all-embracing space. The absence of such a common space would preclude the plenitude of the object – and hence, its very being as an object for consciousness.

In attempting to refute this position, empiricism presupposed its own conclusion that the senses are separate. On the basis of experiments using subjects afflicted with psychic or real blindness it declared, for example, that vision is spatial whereas touch by itself is not. In doing so, the empiricists assumed that the patients' disorder had left their tactile experience unchanged – but this assumption presupposed that the allegedly 'pure data' of each sense can be separated out from the total experience. As Merleau-Ponty points out, no experiment whatsoever can be invoked against the intellectualists' view of the spatiality of the senses, for the simple reason that all experiments already involve an interpretation of the 'facts' which colours the conclusion. The issue must therefore be decided at the level of reflection. The traditional intellectualist reflection however – such as that presented by Kant – is itself based on presuppositions in its thematizing of consciousness and the object. The former, as we have seen, thereby becomes pure being-for-itself while the latter, as pure being-in-itself, becomes universally accessible. But why should we assume that there is such a translucent subject and plenary object, and 'that the world must be capable of being thought' as Kant claims? A genuinely radical reflection is therefore required.

Instead of beginning with an idea of the subject and object, we must return to the pre-reflective experience underlying our ideas and must seek to describe its actual features by our reflection. Kant himself began his *Critique of Pure Reason* with the declaration that 'there can be no doubt that all our knowledge begins with experience'; however, he went on to say that we can 'eliminate from our experiences everything which belongs to the senses' and arrive at 'knowledge absolutely independent of all experience'. This *a priori* knowledge, according to Kant, gives us 'true universality and strict necessity, such as mere empirical knowledge cannot supply'.[1] The phenomenological reflection challenges these claims concerning *a priori* knowledge thus defined, by pointing out that if experience is the start of knowledge – as Kant declared – then it is impossible to distinguish between factual truths and *a priori* truths, between 'what is' and what 'must necessarily be so, and not otherwise'.[2] Prior to this chapter, Merleau-Ponty alerted us to the need to revise our ordinary notions of contingency and necessity; now, he elaborates the phenomenological definition of the *a posteriori* and *a priori* as respectively, 'the isolated and implicit fact' and 'the fact understood, made explicit, and followed through into all the consequences of its latent logic'. The traditional distinction between content and form clearly disappears here and with it, any pretension to a knowledge utterly independent of experience.

Radical reflection thus begins with the recognition of our actual inherence in being. Instead of citing, as does the critical reflection, the conditions which render the world thinkable, the phenomenological reflection expresses our primordial contact with the *de facto* world which envelopes us and which is the only one that can be thought about consequentially. It becomes impossible to cut our knowledge loose from that primordial perceptual experience in which it is rooted; for the phenomenologist there is no necessity external to our senses which dictates their unity. Sensation ceases to be some inert quality or state, or the consciousness of these, and becomes a structure of our being-in-the-world; hence spatiality is inseparable from sensation and it becomes unintelligible to regard any of the senses as non-spatial. Phenomenological reflection on our actual sensory experience reveals the unity and diversity of our senses in that co-existence with the sensible which is prior to any reflection. Instead of positing a single space as the necessary condition which makes qualities thinkable, the radical reflection draws our attention to that lived spatiality which is inseverable from our experience of qualities as particular modes of being-in-the-world. In sensory experience, as we have seen, the sensible beckons to the incarnate subject and the latter responds by shaping existence accordingly, thereby absorbing itself to a greater or lesser degree in one of the senses. The diversity and unity of the senses are thus two aspects of sensing; each sense has its own peculiar world while also gearing into the larger world of our integrated experience.

diversity + unity = two aspects of sensing (each sense has its own world but also gears into the larger world of our integrated experience.

Our rootedness in a single all-embracing space as incarnate subjects opening onto the *de facto* world, is what enables us to shift from the spatiality characterizing one sensory realm to that of another and back again without losing our hold on the world. Thus we can take up our abode in visual space and then, by simply closing our eyes, abandon ourselves to the vastness of auditory space as we settle back to enjoy the symphony in the concert hall, knowing full well that we can move back into visual space when the music ends – or earlier if we so desire. Likewise, blind persons who see for the first time following the removal of their cataracts, thereby enter a visual realm whose spatiality differs from that of the tactile or auditory realms to which they have been accustomed. Yet the interplay of the various senses makes it clear that while each is spatial in a unique way, all contribute to a single comprehensive space. After the cataract operation, convalescents typically initially reach out their hands towards any objects shown them and may try to touch even a sunbeam falling across their pillow. Evidently their tactile experience must be spatial – else they would not reach out to touch whatever is presented; at the same time it is apparent that the structure of their world has differed from that of sighted persons. As they learn to use their eyes, the convalescents bring about a restructuring of their experience and gradually establish an intersensory world in which their vision communicates directly with their touch. In normal experience then, all the senses co-exist and interact so that the contribution of each becomes indistinguishable in the total configuration of perception.

Sensory experience is foreign to natural perception and inherently unstable, insofar as it requires an extremely particularized approach to experience the senses separately or to make a definite sensible quality stand out from the perceptual field. Such an approach makes us oblivious to that 'primary layer' of sensing which is anterior to any separation of the senses. Under the influence of mescalin, this original synaesthetic experience becomes dramatically prominent because the drug prompts its user to suspend that analytic attitude which atomizes the world and instead literally to see sounds, hear colours, and feel these vibrate in his own body. If we insist on retaining the constancy hypothesis (which restricts each stimulus to a single sensation) then such experience remains incomprehensible. Yet we must endeavour to account for it, because synaesthetic perception is not unique to

mescalin users; the scientific attitude of our times has merely
made us unaware that such perception is in fact the rule rather
than the exception. By drawing our attention to the phenomenal
body, which is the actual subject of perception, phenomenological
reflection prompts us to rediscover the true nature of perception
prior to any scientific reconstruction of our experience.

If we suspend objective thought and examine our actual experience, we discover an intercommunication of the senses which
our preconceptions had ruled out. When we consider, for example,
a glass vase, a knife blade, a birch branch, or a fold in red velvet,
we realize that an object's form and the brilliance or dullness of its
colour are indicative of its texture, its flexibility, its warmth or
coldness, its weight, its manner of lending itself to movement, its
sonority when struck, and so on. In its own way, each of the senses
reveals the object's inner core, or structure, and thereby communicates with the other senses as well. However, we must guard
against the temptation to reduce the object's essential nature to a
Kantian noumenon. The perceptual synthesis which accomplishes
the unification of our sensory experiences is fundamentally different from an intellectual synthesis and must not be regarded as
being merely a step on the way to the latter. The perceptual
synthesis is akin to binocular vision's grasp of a single object. Our
actual experience of transferring our gaze from a distant object to
one nearby, shows that binocular vision is neither an automatic
physiological process nor a mental synthesizing of images. The
convergence and merging of two monocular images into the single
object seen, is the outcome of a bodily intentionality; it is the
phenomenal body which experiences diplopia as imbalance and
which focuses its eyes so as to achieve visual equilibrium. It is not
a matter here of an epistemological synthesis effected by a
transparent consciousness. The perceptual synthesis is rooted in
the prelogical unity of the body itself and neither the latter nor the
transcendent object which invites its gaze is ever completely laid
bare. Just as there is no thinking subject which stands behind the
synthesis of double images in normal vision, so there is no
transcendental ego which subsumes the senses and thereby effects
their unity. The unification of the senses comes about through
their ongoing integration into that synergic system which is the
phenomenal body itself. Hearing colours or seeing sounds is no
more – and no less – mysterious or miraculous than is the collaboration of the two eyes in normal vision. As Merleau-Ponty

observes, we can become abruptly aware of the interaction of the senses in perception when the sound of a film we are watching breaks down momentarily, thereby congealing the gestures themselves and altering the whole tenor of the spectacle. The intercommunication of the senses in experience is based on 'a project towards movement' which is inseparable from the very existence of the body itself as primordial expression.

The phenomenal body gives meaning even to cultural objects such as words, as shown by experiments in which subjects who were presented with words too briefly to read them, nevertheless adopted the corresponding bodily attitude. The body thus generally symbolizes the world and enables us to comprehend the latter prior to any conceptualization on our part. At the primary layer of sensing, we discover the unity and opacity of the temporal subject and the intersensory unity of the transcendent object. In accomplishing the perceptual synthesis, the body-subject creates time by bringing a past and future into existence and uniting them with a present. If we are to appreciate the impersonal nature of perception, we must give up the critical attitude which objectifies sensation and purges consciousness of its essential opacity. In place of such intellectualist reflection we must engage in that truly radical reflection which recovers the unreflected experience underlying any positing of object or subject. Such radical reflection recognizes sensation as being 'the most rudimentary of perceptions' and restores it to the perceptual field, while simultaneously reinstating primitive perception as a non-positing, pre-objective, prepersonal experience.

Notes
1. 'Introduction', *Critique of Pure Reason*, Norman Kemp Smith (trans.), (New York: St. Martin's Press, 1965) pp. 41–3.
2. Ibid., p. 42.

2

Space

In the previous chapter, Merleau-Ponty overturned the traditional conception of objectivity by bringing to our attention the phenomenal body as 'a natural self ' and as 'the subject of perception'. We have seen that the experience of the body itself is inseparably the outlining and perceiving of a certain sort of world in which each bodily sense has a spatial realm which overlaps, but does not coincide, with the others. In this chapter, Merleau-Ponty examines more closely the meaning of such spatial realms which form a whole human, or cultural, world around a sensible core.

Traditionally, space has been regarded as a container for, or a common characteristic of, the objects of experience. Alternatively, it has been conceived as the *form* which, constituted by a transcendental subject, makes external experience possible. In short, space has been considered to be either objective or subjective – either part of the 'real' world 'out there', or a principle of unification 'in' the subject of experience. Merleau-Ponty's phenomenological descriptions, however, have revealed that subject to be an incarnate subjectivity rather than a transcendental ego, the subject of experience is the phenomenal body inseparably bound up with the world. It is obvious, therefore, that the traditional notion of space will need to be rethought, and that the unity of experience can no longer be considered to lie 'out there' or 'in here' but must, rather, originates in that dynamic relationship *between* body-subject and world *through* which 'objects' and 'subjects' come into being for us. Consequently, that relationship itself must be pre-objective; and if we wish to retain the terms 'objective' and 'subjective' at this primordial level, we shall have to say that this primary perception is immediately 'subjective–objective' or – which comes to the same thing – 'objective–subjective'. We have become so accustomed to thinking of space in the traditional way, that we require a detailed investigation involving a whole new description of spatiality, in order to break with our entrenched preconceptions. Once again, we will need to question our estab-

80

lished notion of the world and to rediscover the actual pre-reflective experience from which it arises. The final 'court of appeal' concerning the being of space can be no other than our re-awakened experience of space. In our everyday lives, the primordial experience of space is already overlaid by its own acquisitions; hence our investigation must not stop there. If we are to capture the genesis of space, we must consider breakdowns of our normal experience because – as we have seen in earlier chapters – it is in such disturbances that our already constituted world disintegrates, revealing the threads which compose the fabric of our ordinary experience. Merleau-Ponty consequently examines the findings of experiments like those of Stratton, in which special glasses are used to make a subject see without the normal retinal inversion. In this case, the subject initially experiences objects as inverted and unreal, then begins to see objects right-side-up again but experiences his body as inverted, and finally – especially when active – experiences both objects and body as real and right-side-up. What are we to make of these findings?

Neither intellectualism nor empiricism can provide a satisfactory account for Stratton's findings. For the intellectualist, spatial position is simply the result of a transparent constituting activity; hence it lies exclusively on the side of the subject. The intellectualist is therefore at a loss how to explain the subject's actual experience of inversion: since he knows that he is wearing correctional glasses, the subject should (in the intellectualist account) make allowance for this when constituting the form of his visual field. Thus he should continue both to see objects and to experience his body as 'real' and as right-side-up. The empiricist, on the other hand, is at a loss how to explain the fact that everything gradually rights itself even though the subject continues to wear the correctional glasses. According to empiricism everything should remain inverted, since space is a property of the 'real external' world and, as such, impinges on the subject in the same way for the duration of the experiment. Stratton's findings raise a crucial question regarding the meaning of inversion: with reference to *what* does the subject experience the visual field to be either inverted or upright? It will not do to answer that it is the objective body which provides the stable point of orientation, because the body is itself experienced, at least for a time, as inverted. Evidently, space is not simply provided together with the content of sensing; it is neither an objective relationship passively registered by the retina, nor an intellectual construction by a non-spatial ego. The experiment reveals that the content of experience is not orientated in itself; however, if 'up' and 'down' are relative, then to *what* are they relative and how is it that we ever come to experience directions like these at all? What is that 'absolute within the sphere of the relative' which enables the subject of Stratton's experiment to characterizing his own body and his surroundings as either upright or inverted? As Merleau-Ponty points out, this absolute must be a third kind of spatiality underlying any distinction between form and content. Wertheimer's experiment involving a mirror which tilts the room in which a subject is located, shows that directions can be redistributed almost immediately even in the absence of any motor exploration on the part of the subject; and this new orientation is not that of the body axis. In such cases and in general, what counts is not the body as an object occupying objective space; rather, it is the body as potentiality of actions and vehicle of one's being-in-the-world.

The situation and task define the existential 'place' of this phenomenal body; hence, the tilted spectacle rights itself even for an immobile subject as soon as he experiences it as making demands on him. His body gears itself to this new world in such a way that he experiences the former as the comprehensive potentiality of the latter. In short, the subject begins to inhabit his new world and, instead of feeling himself in the world of his actual body, he 'feels that he has the legs and arms he would need to walk and act in the reflected room'. Nagel's experiment with variations in muscular tonicity reveals the other side of this body-subject and world dialectic, by showing that if the spectacle remains stationary while body tonicity is changed, the subject modifies his bodily position accordingly. Instead of a mechanistic deterministic relationship of causality, we have an organic relation of *motivation* between subject and world, such that the body possesses the world in a certain way while gearing itself to that world. In our normal daily experience, our actual body is at one with our virtual body – the latter being the one which the spectacle requires – and the actual spectacle is at one with the setting which our bodily attitude projects around it. Consequently, it is only when one term of the dialectic is upset that the part usually played by both terms becomes visible, revealing simultaneously that direct power which the world holds over our body and the

sens = meaning + direction
is double-sided

reciprocal power which the body has in anchoring itself in a world, in demanding 'certain preferential planes'.

The body is a potentiality of movement, and the perceptual field is an invitation to action; by responding to this invitation, the incarnate subject receives what Merleau-Ponty calls 'the enjoyment of space' through the existential constitution of 'a spatial level'. The criterion for this dialectic lies in the 'maximum sharpness of perception and action'; hence, the utmost possible variation and clarity of articulation in the spectacle perceived, and the world's confirmation of the body's unfolding motor intentions, indicate the gearing of the body to the world. This reciprocal hold of the body on the world and the world on the body, is that perceptual ground, that absolute within relativity, from which particular directions like 'up' and 'down' ultimately spring. To ask *why* clarity and richness of perception and action require an orientated phenomenal space, is to adopt the position of a non-situated spectator floating somewhere above a world in itself already absolutely orientated. This sort of question presupposes that subject and world are essentially indifferent to space and merely happen to be orientated. In fact, however, our perceptual experience discloses that to be is to be situated; that our primordial co-existence with the world 'magnetizes' experience and induces a direction in it. The double meaning of the French word *sens* is significant in this connection: if there is to be meaning, there must be direction; meaning and direction go hand in hand. By virtue of being incarnate subjectivities, we thus always already find ourselves in a world which is primordially meaningful prior to any explicit taking of a stand by the personal self.

We saw in the last chapter that objectivity has its genesis in a pre-objective dialectic which overturns the traditional conceptions; and it now becomes evident that this coming to be of objectivity is the coming to be of orientated being. To be an object is to be such for a bodily gaze or grip. Spatial direction is not a merely contingent trait of an object but rather, the means for recognizing it and being conscious of it as an object. This is so because the subject of perception is the phenomenal body, which can structure the world into figure–background configurations only insofar as it has a grip on things – and this taking of a grip is possible only insofar as things have a general direction. All perceivable and all conceivable being (the latter always based on the former) is orientated; we can never get beyond orientated

The enjoyment of space

Trad. view unpacked

The body as generalized, natural self (anonymous body) =
The customary, habitual body
↳ our facticity

84   *Part II: The Perceived World*

being in order to provide it with a non-orientated foundation. Our express perception can never reach and thematize that primordial laying down of directions whereby we become situated in the world. To be aware of ourselves as incarnate subjectivity is always to find ourselves already situated – that is, already orientated. Reflection invariably encounters a spatiality which is already acquired, indicating that there must be a pre-personal existence underlying our personal history. This pre-reflective existence can only be that of our body as a generalized, anonymous, natural self. Of course, this is not that 'momentary body' of our personal decisions but rather, the 'customary' or 'habitual body' of which Merleau-Ponty has already had occasion to speak. The primordial communication with the world which the habitual body inaugurates and perpetuates, opens up a realm of freedom and a specifically human world in which reflection can take up its abode. Yet that primordial contact itself, being nothing other than our facticity, remains radically impenetrable for reflection.

Merleau-Ponty's disclosure of primordial spatiality as inseparable from our very being in the world, enables us to comprehend why the awareness of our contingency prompts giddiness, loss of secure foundations, horror, nausea (as described in Sartre's famous novel of the same title) and – if it engulfs us sufficiently long – the schizophrenia which finds everything 'amazing, absurd, or unreal'. Between the disorientation of madness and the unquestioned security of the natural attitude to the world, lies the realm of philosophical interrogation which attempts to understand both without succumbing to either. The natural attitude of course is not entirely closed in upon itself – if it were, interrogation could never even begin. Now in the case of spatiality, philosophical interrogation finds for its inquiry a foothold, so to speak, in the notion of depth. As Merleau-Ponty points out, depth is more 'existential' than the other spatial dimensions because it clearly is neither simply a property of the object nor an intellectual construct; therefore its consideration prompts us more directly to repudiate our preconceived notions and re-discover the primordial experience of the world.

depth

Traditional theories attempted to reduce depth to breadth seen from the side, but this so to speak 'flattened it out' and failed to account for our lived experience of depth. Even these traditional theories thus could not dispense with the notions of distance, relationship, size and motion in their analyses of depth. To say

The momentary body = the reflective body of our personal decision
It takes up its residence in the habitual, customary body

that depth is merely breadth seen from the side, is to acknowledge that the breadth is further away from me when I take a frontal view of the object in question. Even here therefore, distance from a perceiver is already included. Moreover, if we ask how we become aware of distance, the reply will be that objects change in apparent size as they *move* closer to or further away from us. Here, just as in the case of verticality, the question of an absolute criterion arises: with reference to *what* are objects to be judged bigger or smaller? It cannot simply be a matter of ascertaining size with reference to other objects in our visual field, for that would involve us in an infinite regress. As Merleau-Ponty shows, the absolute here is that which our earlier discussion of space already revealed to us – namely, that 'gearing of body-subject and world which brings about the maximum richness and clarity of perception. Distance is not an external relationship between things; rather, it is a dialectical relationship between the phenomenal body and its world. To say that something is close, is to say that the body has a 'full' or 'complete' grip on it; to say that it is further away is to say that it is slipping from our grip; and to say that it is distant, is to say that our gaze now has merely a 'loose and approximate grip' on it, such that the object's richness is no longer clearly articulated and that it lends itself less to our exploration. In this lived distance, motion and temporality are already implied insofar as the body is a power of exploration. To say that something is either no longer or not yet clearly visible, is to invoke temporal horizons of past and future around a field of presence; and it is to disclose the overlapping, interlocking style of being which characterizes these temporal dimensions. To say that something becomes smaller or larger, increasingly indeterminate or determinate, only makes sense if that thing has an identity – if it is not a matter of constant creation *ex nihilo* or radical disappearance. Merleau-Ponty therefore examines the traditional accounts of motion, for it is motion which encompasses simultaneously position, temporality and identity.

The examination of the classical logical and psychological conceptions of motion reveals a more primordial, pre-objective motion which is nothing other than a variation of the phenomenal body's hold on the world. Since primordial spatiality is that pre-objective experience in which the body-subject fastens itself on to its environment, and since primordial motility is a modality of that grip on the world, it becomes evident that spatiality and

Primordial spatiality → pre-objective fastening of the body onto its environment
Primordial motility → a modality of its grip on the world

motility are internally related, being mutually implicatory. The birth of movement for us is part of the genesis of the phenomenal world; consequently, the phenomenological description of the latter involves that of the former. As usual, the shortcoming of the traditional approaches lies in their uncritical acceptance of the prejudice of the objective world. In the case of the logicians, it is a matter of presupposing an object in-itself which remains the same while moving from one objective location to another. On this account, motion is merely an intellectual judgement and Zeno's famous paradoxes become unavoidable. We have a perception of a static object occupying successive positions but never really moving. And yet, we actually have an experience of movement when we dance or walk or use our body in some other way; hence movement cannot be merely an addition of static points in space and time. The logician argues that the perception of movement requires an external landmark relative to which an object is judged to be in motion – that is, to change its position. However, our own pre-reflective bodily experience of motion refutes the logician's claim. My body is not for me an object in-itself; I cannot jump outside it in order to see it occupy successive positions in objective space. Stroboscopic movement also discloses that the perception of movement does not require an identical moving object or an external landmark. The psychologist therefore maintains that the awareness of 'global movement' involves neither a moving object nor a particular position of such an object. Yet in discarding all identity and all relativity, the psychologist forgets that motion is perceived by someone who lives through it.

The perception of movement cannot entirely dispense with the notion of identity; but the latter is not the identity of an already totally determinate object underlying the phases of motion. Movement is not an accidental property of an essentially static object; instead, there is a mobile being whose identity lies in the movement rather than beneath it. As Merleau-Ponty notes, 'it is not because I find the same stone on the ground that I believe in its identity throughout its movement. It is, on the contrary, because I perceived it as identical during that movement . . . that I go to pick it up and recover it'. This identity is pre-objective; it is not the persistence of a cluster of determinate attributes, but a style of existence characterizing a pre-objective entity which is experienced by a relative, pre-personal subject. Relativity here must not be supposed to indicate an external relationship between two terms, it being a matter of indifference which term is varied. Motion is, rather, a structural phenomenon having to do with the articulation of our perceptual field into figure–background; and the *way* in which the body, as subject of perception, establishes its relation with the world is what determines part of the perceptual field to count as the background and another part to count as a moving object. The context in which the phenomenal body anchors itself and which it inhabits, becomes the background against which movement can stand out; consequently, movement presupposes that inherence in the world which is established and maintained by the habitual body. It is this pre-logical gearing of subject and world which provides the foundation for the absolute or 'global movement' depicted by the psychologist – but the latter's prejudice precludes the recognition of this 'primordial anchorage'.

The anchoring of the body as a 'natural self' institutes a physical or 'natural' space and thereby opens up a 'human space' which encompasses the world of emotions, dreams, myths and madness, as well as the world of reflection. The description of this human space overturns our traditional distinctions – such as those between form and content, clarity and ambiguity, reality and appearance – and revolutionizes the role of philosophy itself.

3
The Thing and the
Natural World

We saw in the last chapter that space has traditionally been considered to be a form generated by the subject as the condition of there being any objects at all; or, on the realist side, that it has been regarded as a giant container in which things are located. Merleau-Ponty rejected both these traditional conceptions of space and described the genesis of space in a dynamic pre-objective, pre-logical interaction of body-subject and world. The foundation or ground of spatiality therefore shifted from the constituting activity of a transcendental ego posited by intellectualism, to the reciprocal hold of the phenomenal body and world as described by phenomenology. It emerged that objects are neither purely constructed by the subject nor simply encountered as absolutely independent existents. Rather, there is a genesis of objectivity in an anonymous body–world dialectic, such that objectivity comes to be only as orientated being for a bodily gaze or 'grip'. In short, we saw that lived spatiality is inseparable from objectivity, since such spatiality is the means whereby we recognize and are aware of objects as objects. We saw that objects are always objects for us – but that this 'us' refers first and foremost to the body as natural self and subject of perception, through whose activity objects come into being.

Since the traditional conceptions of space as transcendental form or in-itself container have been thus overturned, it is encumbent on Merleau-Ponty to give an account now of that which was encompassed by, or contained in, the traditional space. The conception of the world as a totality of things contained in space will therefore need to be questioned – and what better way to begin this interrogation than by examining what it means to be a thing? Merleau-Ponty's rejection of the traditional conceptions of objectivity and his attempt to develop a new approach to it in his descriptions of sensing and space, would seem at first glance to rule out objectivity or 'thinghood' altogether. Has Merleau-Ponty destroyed the independence of the thing and absorbed it into the subject of perception by making objectivity the outcome of a body–world dialectic whose foundation is the body-subject's power of anchoring itself in a pre-objective world through the exercise of its sensory organs? In having collapsed the notion of space as transcendental form or in-itself container, has he not in fact collapsed everything in that container and precluded the unity and objectivity of the world? In having rejected the notion of identity as a collection of determinate characteristics which persist as properties of the thing despite contingent changes of time or place, and in having described identity as a dynamic 'style of existence', has Merleau-Ponty not sacrificed the very existence of anything whatsoever? Has he not substituted a radical subjectivism in place of the traditional positions? Merleau-Ponty himself is only too aware of such questions and the dangers to which they refer. In this chapter he therefore addresses himself directly to dispelling such fears.

Traditionally, 'things' have been considered to have stable properties which give them their reality as things. If, for example, a tree twig is put under a magnifying glass, or dropped into a glass of water, or flooded with red light we say that it appears successively as huge, bent, and strangely dark or coloured. Despite these appearances, we say that 'in reality' the twig is tiny, straight and dull brown; in other words, it has its size, its shape, its colour, all of which remain despite the apparent changes brought on by the magnifying glass, water, and coloured light. Once these are removed, the twig can again be seen as it 'really' or 'truly' is; in short, the thing which we call 'the real twig' is considered to have a constancy of size, shape, colour, and so on. Merleau-Ponty therefore sets himself the task of describing the phenomenon of reality via a phenomenological investigation of the phenomenon of perceptual constancy. As usual, he proceeds by examining the traditional approaches to the question.

Psychology considers 'constant' or 'true' size and shape to be a convention, arguing that no single size and shape is truer than others, since they all vary according to one's perspective. For the sake of convenience, it is simply agreed that the object's size when it is within reach, and its shape when it is in a plane paralleling the frontal elevation, will be called its 'true' or 'real' size and shape. However, despite the fact that psychology acknowledges the body's active role in the production of sizes and shapes, this sort of approach presupposes precisely what needs to be examined. Psychology begins with the assumption that the given is a collection of already determinate sizes and shapes, and then tries to explain why a particular one is regarded as 'real' or 'constant' in preference to all the others. Yet what needs to be shown is how a determinate size or shape can become crystallized in our experience – that is, how constancy comes into being for us, or in short, how there can be objectivity at all. It should be noted here that the question is not *why*, but *how*; for to ask why our experience crystallizes at all, would be to adopt an acosmic stance and pretend that experience would still be experience in the absence of all objectivity. Merleau-Ponty has already criticized this sort of question – most recently, in his discussion of space, where the questioner assumes that orientation is merely an accidental attribute. The psychologist presupposes objectivity and hence fails to describe its genesis in our lived experience.

The intellectualist's approach fares no better than does the psychologist's. In an effort to avoid the latter's problem of deciding which of a whole series of appearances is to be called the object's reality, intellectualism tries to evade the issue of objectivity altogether. Instead of underlying the object's various appearances, the 'real' object is considered to be the totality of all its actual and possible appearings. Thus, to appear is to be – being is appearing; however, this is not a reduction to any single appearance but rather, the sum total of all possible appearances as these are foreshadowed in any actual, specific appearance. By thus collapsing the distinction between the object and its appearances, intellectualism renders appearance as appearance imcomprehensible.

In its attempt to get beyond the traditional dichotomies of crude realism, it becomes itself enmeshed in an infinite regress, as Sartre explained in *Being and Nothingness*.[1] What, after all, is it that is appearing? What is the being of that appearing? Is it an appearing? If so, then what is the being of *that* appearing? The intellectualist thus gets caught in this infinite regress and never manages to show what it is to *appear*. Nevertheless, this position has a positive insight in stipulating that there is a 'tightly knit system' of phenomena and the body, and that shape and size have to do with 'the relations between the parts of the phenomenal field'. However, intellectualism distorts this insight by conceiving these relations as being mental ones; thus it considers the constancy of real size or shape to be merely an *a priori* law governing the variations of apparent size relative to apparent distance. In treating appearance, distance, and orientation as variables in a constant law, the intellectualist assumes that these are already determinate; consequently, intellectualism brings us no further in understanding how determinate shapes and sizes come into being for us.

By reducing perception to thought, intellectualism blinds itself to our pre-scientific experience and fails to account for it – while covertly presupposing that pre-thetic experience in its own analyses. More specifically, it cannot account for our actual experience of perceiving the object either far away or up close. Intellectualism is forced to regard an apparently small object at a great distance as indistinguishable from the same object seen up close as large, because for it the object is the constant product of the apparent size multiplied by the distance. Yet in our lived experience, the object at a distance is not as real and present as it is when close to us. Far from a neutral ratio, our lived experience reveals distance as tension, orientation (of the object) as the balance between inner and outer horizons, and variations in appearance as articulation. Intellectualism cannot account for the experience of tension, or imbalance or unclarity; nor can it make comprehensible the fact that there is one culminating point of the perceptual process 'which simultaneously satisfies these three norms'. According to the intellectualist position, no one perception is more crucial than any other; hence there can be no optimum distance and orientation which provide the perceiver with maximum visibility. Nonetheless, we know perfectly well that when looking at pictures in an art gallery, for example, we move forward or backward a few paces for each picture which we really wish to view. Our body here understands that there is for each picture an optimum distance and direction from which to see it. As usual, moreover, the intellectualist approach reverses the actual relationship of '*Fundierung*'; thus it reduces the thing to constant relationships, instead of recognizing that the latter are themselves based on the perceptual self-evidence of the thing. It is the thing's self-evidence in our lived experience which must therefore be described.

We have already seen that the primordial ground of spatial directions lies in the comprehensive, reciprocal hold of the phenomenal body and the world. This anchoring of the body-subject in a world, and the anonymous body–world dialectic to which it ceaselessly gives rise, is the source of objectivity. Since we are involved in the world through our body, the appearance of objects is always inseparable from a particular bodily attitude. The constancy of things can no longer be regarded as a mechanical or intellectual function, but must be acknowledged to be inseparable from the fundamental dialectic whereby the incarnate subject assumes his place in the world. There is a *telos* or decisive perception in the perceptual process precisely because that process has to do with the way in which the body gears itself to the world so that, as Merleau-Ponty says, 'sizes and shapes merely provide a modality for this comprehensive hold on the world. The thing is big if my gaze cannot fully take it in, small if it does so easily'. In the past chapter, we saw that things appear unreal when the primordial, anonymous body–world dialectic is disturbed with the aid of correctional glasses or mirrors, and that reality is re-established when the body adjusts its hold on the world in accordance with the requirements of the altered situation. It is this comprehensive grip on the world which brings a perceptual field into being, so that the anchoring of the body-subject in the world is simultaneously finitude, incompleteness, and openness. In short, to have a hold on an object through one's comprehensive grip on the world, is to be perspectival – though not sealed into any particular perspective, because one is a comprehensive power of world-modalities (that is, a power of ceaselessly modifying the specific forms which that primordial hold of the body on the world takes). In the present chapter, Merleau-Ponty enéavours to show that the self-evidence – and hence the constancy – of things is rooted in that of the body itself as a comprehensive hold on a world.

A thing's constancy has to do not only with its size and shape, but also with features such as colour; hence it is important to consider what it means for a colour to be 'real'. What does it mean to say that an object has its own colour, which it retains throughout 'apparent' transformations brought about by changes in position or lighting, for example? It is not enough to say that the 'real' or 'constant' colour of an object is simply that colour which it 'normally' assumes – in daylight, at a certain distance, etc. – and that the perceiver remembers this colour when viewing the object under other conditions. This sort of position again presupposes precisely that which calls for elucidation; namely, how a colour comes to crystallize in our experience at all. The appeal to memory assumes that determinate colours are given, and chooses one of these to be consigned to memory for future reference. Such a procedure once more reduces perception to thought about perception – and from our earlier discussion we are already acquainted with the fallacies involved in adopting this kind of approach. In reducing colour to a fixed quality, empiricism and intellectualism both distort the phenomenon of colour in our experience. Colour constancy is not a matter of such a *quale* constructed by reflection *post facto*; rather, it has to do with a colour-function. The latter is not an incidental coating added to a colourless substratum; it is, instead, the way in which the thing draws the incarnate subject's gaze, the sort of resistance which it offers to visual exploration. Physics and psychology have distorted this colour-function by dissecting colour into 'atoms' or 'patches' of colour. It is true that we can see coloured areas by squinting our eyes or engaging in experimental manipulations of vision; however, the colour-function changes in such cases so that the objectivity, or reality, of the coloured thing is lost. Besides, coloured areas are only one of the many possible structures of colour – others, such as glow, gloss, the colour of transparent things or of lighting, are omitted in such an account of colour. No more than spatial direction is colour an inert component of an absolute object. To show this, Merleau-Ponty embarks on a detailed discussion of lighting.

Lighting has usually been regarded as something essentially insubstantial, while colour has been considered part of an object in itself. However, traditional painting reveals that lighting itself solidifies into a thing as soon as it is focused upon instead of being taken for granted. If it is to function as lighting, it must not itself be the object of our gaze but rather, that which draws our gaze in such a way as to see the rest. In the previous chapter, we saw that in order to apprehend movement, the perceiver must focus on the figures rather than on the background of his phenomenal field. We see now that the reverse is true of the structure lighting-object lighted: in order to apprehend lighting as lighting, the perceiver must not seize on it with his gaze, but must allow it to stay in the background. In its function as lighting, light has a direction and meaning ('sens') which the body understands and to which it responds without any need for reflection. Merleau-Ponty showed in his earlier discussion of speech that meaning is not a property of discrete words or speech elements but rather, that words have a meaning only insofar as they form part of an organically related system. The same is true of colour: things have a colour not because they are isolated in-itselfs, but because they are essentially related to one another as parts of a perceptual field.

Already in the 'Preface' and the 'Introduction' to his *Phenomenology*, Merleau-Ponty pointed out that perception as such requires figure–background articulations; moreover, from the last chapter we know that such articulations involve spatial dimensions like depth, which have their source in the lived spatiality of the phenomenal body. In the present chapter, we become aware of the role played by lighting in the articulation of the perceptual field. Lighting is that which enables coloured things to stand out, or figure, in our vision; hence it is itself prior to 'the distinction between colours and luminosities' (being that whereby these come into being for us). In the previous chapter, we saw that the distortions of spatiality induced by glasses or mirrors do not cease to be distorting until the subject begins to inhabit the new spectacle through the adjusting of spatial levels. The same applies now to lighting: to function as such, lighting must cease to be an object confronting us and become instead our environment in which we take up our position. When lighting is allowed to function in this manner, a new colour level is established. If we switch on our electric lamp, the light initially appears yellow; however, it soon assumes the function of lighting and thus creates a 'new atmosphere' in which colours are distributed in accordance with the degree and kind of resistance which the various objects offer. A blue paper looks blue in gaslight even though it transmits exactly the same mixture of rays to the retina as are transmitted in daylight by a brown paper. Far from being given as fixed qualities, colours come to be determinate in relation to a level constituted by the phenomenon of lighting; moreover, that level is itself variable, being the structuring of our visual field in one of a whole variety of ways.

The genesis of determinate colours therefore depends on colour-functions which enable colours to *become* determinate in relation to a level of lighting. As Merleau-Ponty stresses, 'the level is laid down, and with it all the colour values dependent upon it, as soon as we begin to live in the prevailing atmosphere and re-allot to objects the colours of the spectrum in accordance with the requirements of this basic convention'. The only way of inhabiting this new setting is through 'a bodily operation' which directs our gaze, via the agency of lighting, in such a way that we apprehend the thing as 'real'. Lighting endows things with their 'true' colours through an interaction of all parts of the visual field; consequently, lighting is not incidental, but essential to vision. The 'logic of lighting' is what makes possible the emergence of a coherent spectacle.

We have seen that colour is not first and foremost a determinate quality, but the way in which an object modulates light in coming into being as an object for us. Since such modulation has to do with a total configuration involving all the other objects in our visual field, it is clear that colour constancy is inseparable from the constancy of things and, further, from 'the primordial constancy of the world' as the horizon of our visual field and, of course, of all our experiences. Colour constancy – and more generally, perceptual constancy – is not a matter of a thing's possessing stable characteristics. Rather, it is that self-evidence in which the thing as 'intersensory unity' speaks to our perceptual powers in such a way that we, as incarnate subjectivities, understand its style in an apprehension which simultaneously gives us a certain clarity and a certain richness of perceptual detail. In order to appreciate the significance of this conclusion, we must consider more closely the meaning of modulating light.

We have seen that Merleau-Ponty speaks of this modulation in terms of the *resistance* which the object offers to light. It is therefore readily understandable that the modulation of light, which brings about the structuration of a visual field, has to do with the texture of the thing. Colour and texture are consequently inseparable; the visual and tactile powers of the perceiving subject are mutually implicatory and gear into one another. In the case of touch, the part played by movement and time is more apparent than in the case of vision, because in seeing we have the illusion of attaining everything simultaneously and instantaneously – whereas in touching we are aware of the time unfolded in the movement of our hand over the tactile object. It is important to notice, moreover, that the notion of resistance already implies the other sensory realms as well – for example, the thing's texture offers a certain resistance to sound (muffled or not) and connotes a certain smell and taste. In short, the thing has an intersensory unity corresponding to that synthetic totality of sensory powers which *is* the incarnate subject. That balance of clarity and richness which we encountered with reference to vision, must therefore be extended to include the other sensibilities. Thus the thing is self-evident or 'real' when the body, as comprehensive synthesis of intersensory powers, has a hold on the thing as intersensory object. There is therefore a general perceptual optimum which has to do with the balance of clarity and richness in all the sensory fields as they gear into one another.

Finally, it should be noted that although the thing is inseparable from the perceiver – being constituted as a thing in the latter's grip on the world – nevertheless, it is a thing in-itself for us. The thing has a resistance, indicating a non-human core which prevents its ever being absorbed into the perceiving subject. If we take seriously the various sensory resistances of the thing discussed above, as well as the intersensory unity of the thing, then we will have no difficulty in countering idealism. Further, we must dispense with that prejudice according to which objectivity is equated with completeness. The coming into being of the thing for the perceiver involves a modulation which is incomprehensible in the absence of time. Merleau-Ponty therefore shows that the thing's objectivity is inseparable from its open-ended nature, and hence also from that fundamental ambiguity which is involved in the richness of perception.

Notes
1.   Sartre, 'Introduction': 'The Pursuit of Being', *Being and Nothingness: a Phenomenological Essay on Ontology*, Hazel Barnes (trans.), (New York: Washington Square Press, 1966) pp. 3ff.

4

Others and the Human World*

In the previous chapters of this part of the *Phenomenology*, Merleau-Ponty has presented a detailed phenomenological description of the genesis of objectivity. We have seen that far from being given, objectivity comes into being through a body–world dialogue whose foundation is the body-subject's primordial power of anchoring itself in a pre-objective world through the exercise of its sensory organs. We have seen that things become 'real' when the body-subject, as a comprehensive intersensory power, has a grip on them as intersensory objects. We have seen that this 'hold' involves a gearing of the body to the world and moreover, that it implies motion, temporality, incompleteness and ambiguity. We have seen that although things are inseparable from the perceiver, being constituted in the latter's hold on the world, they are nonetheless objective. Things thus have an independence – but not an absolute independence; they are in-themselves for us. Things have a constancy, an identity; yet we have seen that it is not a matter of their possessing stable inert properties. Rather, the thing's identity is a dynamic 'style of existence' which emerges in the way in which that thing invites, and responds to, perceptual exploration. Thus colour, for example, is not a fixed quality; instead, colour constancy has to do with the manner in which the thing draws the body-subject's gaze and the kind of resistance it offers to visual exploration. We have seen that the thing's way of modulating light is also indicative of its texture, its flexibility, its weight, and its sonority when struck. The thing 'speaks' to the various sensory powers without ever collapsing into the perceiver; objectivity and perceptual experience are simultaneously inseparable and irreducible. Thing and perceiver

---

* In an effort to remain as close as possible to the original text, I am translating 'Autrui' as 'Others', rather than as 'Other Selves'.

gear into one another without either becoming absorbed into the other. Far from being found ready-made, determinate sizes, shapes and colours come into being from a general atmosphere established by those 'levels' which the body-subject lays down in taking anchorage in a world. The emergence of objectivity requires the inhabiting of this general atmosphere by the 'natural self '. Since our perception is not restricted to things and the natural world, however, it is not enough to show that objectivity is the outcome of a pre-personal dialogue whose terms are the phenomenal body and the pre-objective world. In this final chapter of 'The Perceived World', Merleau-Ponty therefore examines our perception of others and the cultural world. It is now a question of describing the genesis of subjectivity – that is, of showing how specifically cultural objects and other people come into being for us, how they manifest themselves in our re-awakened experience. We will find the same basic features in the phenomenon of subjectivity that we have already discovered in the phenomenon of objectivity; and if we have understood the latter, then the former will not pose any difficulty for us. The transition is readily apparent: we are proceeding from a consideration of how we perceive objects, to a consideration of how we perceive cultural objects – how, despite their 'non-human core', objects can manifest an element of humanity. This will bring us to the more general question of how humanity comes into being for us – that is, how other subjectivities make their appearance in our experience.

Traditionally, the entire issue has been dealt with as 'the problem of other minds'; and in the very way in which this has been phrased we can already detect the source of the dilemmas to which it has given rise. If subjectivity is reduced to mind – or constituting consciousness – then the existence of any subjectivity other than one's own becomes utterly incomprehensible. It is of no avail to protest that the ego can posit other consciousnesses as simultaneously engaged in constituting the world; for its very positing of those consciousnesses renders the ego supreme by collapsing the others into mere moments of its own activity. Solipsism is therefore the price one pays for reducing subjectivity to mind which, as a constituting consciousness, is characterized by transparency and completeness. However, solipsism is an untenable position because its very articulation requires the use of an intersubjective language which belies the claims it is propounding. Besides, the pre-reflective experience and the behaviour of the declared solipsist continually subvert his alleged solipsism – thereby making it not only an untenable position but also a dishonest one, insofar as it always already surreptitiously presupposes that which it attempts to deny.

How, then, has traditional philosophy tried to account for our actual experience of living in a world with other subjectivities? The typical approach has been to invoke the 'argument from analogy', according to which I deduce the existence of others from the behaviour of the bodies which I perceive, by reasoning via analogy from the correlation between my own 'conscious states' and the behaviour of my body.[1] As we might expect, there are several problems in seeking to base intersubjectivity on analogy. Since the argument is predicated on the old mind–body dualism, it falls prey to all the difficulties of dualism which Merleau-Ponty has already discussed in detail in his earlier chapters. At the core of these difficulties, as we have seen, is the lack of any common ground between consciousness conceived as pure 'for-itself ' and body considered as pure 'in-itself '; moreover, the argument from analogy presupposes what it sets itself to explain. The argument is formulated in language and presented for someone; hence, it tacitly presupposes the existence of others. In addition, the comparison of others' emotional expressions with our own assumes that self-perception is anterior to, and the basis for, the perception of others; yet the reverse is in fact the case. Consequently, self-perception cannot serve as the foundation for an argument about the existence of 'other minds'. Merleau-Ponty's reference to the behaviour of small children is especially relevant here. As he points out, a fifteen-month-old baby opens its own mouth if someone pretends to bite one of its fingers. Clearly, it is not a matter of the baby's first perceiving its own expression on the occasion of intending to bite something, then perceiving the expression of the body whose mouth is moving towards its finger, and finally, reasoning by analogy that there is behind this approaching mouth a consciousness with intent to bite. Instead of such an elaborate reasoning procedure by a transparent, self-sufficient consciousness, we have here an incarnate subject who, as incarnate intentionality, perceives other incarnate intentionalities directly because it and they are internally related.

In the chapter 'The Body as Expression and Speech', we saw that intentions are not mental entities essentially independent of a mechanistic body; we discovered instead a bodily intentionality which 'speaks to' other phenomenal bodies and is comprehended by them prior to any reflection on either side. Thus in the present example, the baby does not thematize its own intentions but perceives them directly in its body – it simply feels its mouth as an apparatus for biting. By the same token, the baby neither posits the existence of others nor deduces their intentions by analogy with its own; rather, it perceives others' bodies with its own phenomenal body and thereby directly perceives their intentions. Others' intentions and its own form a single pre-reflective inter-subjective system in which there is no need for any translation. Of course, it is always possible for the adult to engage in reasoning by analogy; but such reasoning is the exception rather than the norm and is employed precisely when the intersubjective world some-how breaks down or is deliberately put in abeyance. For the child, there is no 'problem of other minds' because the intersubjective world is self-evident; in fact, the child's experience is at the opposite extreme insofar as he is totally oblivious to the perspec-tivity of incarnate consciousness and to the meaning of private subjectivity. It is important therefore to describe the genesis of subjectivity in terms of the emergence of human personality from that pre-personal existence of the body which is its foundation.

The notion of 'body image' plays a crucial role in the phenome-nological description of the pre-personal realm of our existence. As we saw in the first part of the *Phenomenology*, classical psychology has employed the term to designate a representation of the various points of the body as a system of externally related parts (*'partes extra partes'*); however, this mechanistic conception proved to be at odds with our actual experience as highlighted by the breakdowns which Merleau-Ponty considered. Consequently, the notion of body image had to undergo a radical transformation involving a distinction between the 'customary' or 'habitual body' and the body lived at a particular moment on the basis of such an acquired body. Thus the habitual modes of interacting with the world were shown to sediment themselves in the body and become that crucial acquisition without which the freedom that is characteristic of personal existence would be precluded. For phe-nomenology, the body image was not a mental representation of the physiological body considered as a mechanistic system merely externally related to its environment. On the contrary, phenomenology disclosed the body image as the pre-personal awareness of the phenomenal body polarized by the world of its habitual tasks. In the present chapter, we see that this revised body image encompasses not only the natural world, but also other human beings and the cultural world.

The child is already situated in an intersubjective cultural world and from infancy on develops habitual modes of relating to this human world through his bodily powers. It is in and through such pre-reflective interaction that the child gradually develops a concept of subjectivity. Language is an important part of this human world and the child appropriates it before ever using it consciously to articulate his selfhood. Further, as Merleau-Ponty emphasizes here, pre-personal existence – whether that of the child developing into a person or that of the adult situating himself in the pre-reflective realm of his tasks – is characterized by dialogue. Others and the cultural world become part of the body image and are understood prior to any reflection. We have already seen that the body is primordially expressive, and it is so by and for human beings. It is the phenomenal body which comprehends, appropriates, and sediments the human world into its own dynamic structure. Moreover, the apprehension of the intersubjective world poses no more problem at the pre-reflective level than does the apprehension of one's own limbs; for just as the body's different sensory realms gear into one another and open onto an intersensory field, so the intersensory fields of different individuals gear into each other and open onto an intersubjective world. Since personal existence, being inherently temporal, is fraught with ambiguity and opacity, the opacity and ambiguity of interpersonal life should come as no surprise. Just as I am outrun by my own past and future and supported by an anonymous bodily existence, or 'natural self ', so too I am outrun by others and they by me. Thus the 'kernel of truth' in the solipsist position is that of non-coincidence – I am unable ever to coincide with others, to experience their experiences as they themselves do. But on the other hand, I never entirely coincide with myself either, because self-awareness on principle implies a distancing and because my own experiences are continually remade by time. All attempts to reconstruct my own past as I actually lived it, are doomed to failure; henceforth that past eludes me and can exist only in an 'ambiguous presence'. Yet in both cases – and this is what the solipsist fails to acknowledge – I am essentially open; I am open to my own past and to other people, I exist with others in a common world in which my experience interweaves with theirs.

It should be noted that the refutation of solipsism does not in and of itself suffice to establish this primordial reciprocity with others in an 'interworld' which we all inhabit. Sartre, for example, rejects solipsism but presents a phenomenological description of our 'concrete relations with others' which contrasts sharply with that provided by Merleau-Ponty. Sartre declares that the experience of conflict with the other is the basis of our consciousness of others. Far from being 'an ontological structure of human-reality', the experience of being-with-others (the 'we') is merely 'a certain particular experience which is produced in special cases' and is based on the prior experience of being objectified by others or of objectifying them by our look. The experience of community is an inherently unstable and derivative experience for Sartre, and it is significant that he considers 'the best example of the "we" [to] be furnished us by the spectator at a theatrical performance' who is non-thetically aware of 'being a *co-spectator* of the spectacle'. Sartre concludes that 'the very nature of the We-subject implies that it is made up of only fleeting experiences without metaphysical bearing'; that the experience of being with others is a 'fragmentary, strictly psychological' experience which 'reveals nothing particular; it is a purely subjective *Erlebnis*' rather than 'the revelation of a dimension of real existence'. In short, according to Sartre it is 'useless for human-reality to seek to get out of this dilemma: one must either transcend the Other or allow oneself to be transcended by him. The essence of the relations between consciousnesses is not the *Mitsein*; it is conflict'.[2]

For Merleau-Ponty, it is on the contrary the experience of conflict which is derivative, while that of community has ontological priority and indeed reveals an essential dimension of our real existence as we have seen. Merleau-Ponty points out (without mentioning Sartre by name) that the 'inhuman gaze' by which others objectify me, and I them, presupposes our withdrawing from our pre-reflective inter-active presence, 'into the core of our thinking nature' and into an 'inactive' existence. This withdrawal is experienced as such; thereby confirming the existence of that which it has chosen to abandon. Thus the alienating look of the other disturbs me, whereas the gaze of a dog or cat does not, precisely because the former replaces potential communication with a repudiation, which itself remains 'a form of communication'. The source of this fundamental difference between the position of Sartre and that of Merleau-Ponty, lies in the former's failure to provide any 'third term' between consciousness and being (between 'le néant' or 'pour-soi', and 'l'être' or 'en-soi').[3] Sartre ultimately misses the phenomenon of incarnate subjectivity – that inherence of consciousness in the body and the world which is the central theme of Merleau-Ponty's entire *Phenomenology*.

In the absence of such a body-subject, Sartre cannot establish that bodily intentionality which links my experience dialectically with that of another body-subject so that we are able to find the prolongation and fulfilment of our intentions in each other prior to any reflection and thereby become mutually enriched. Merleau-Ponty's phenomenological description of the body and of the perceived world constitutes a refutation of the kind of view which Sartre presents regarding my perception of the other's body and the nature of our relationship. Sartre must therefore be considered wrong in claiming that the primary relation is not one between my body and that of the other; that such an inter-corporeal relation would be 'purely external'; that the other's body is merely 'a secondary structure' for me, an 'episode' in my project of 'making an object of the Other'; that 'the Other's body is . . . the tool which I am not and which I utilize (or which resists me, which amounts to the same thing). It is presented to me originally with a certain objective coefficient of utility and of adversity'.[4]

Merleau-Ponty's phenomenological description does not, of course, rule out the possibility of utilizing the other's body as a mere tool; however, that possibility is based on a prior development of subjectivity through a sustained interaction of an entirely different sort with other people. I am not first and foremost a spectacle for an alien consciousness, or a spectator of others; rather, as a body-subject I enjoy an anterior organic relationship to the natural and the human world. My body's insertion into the world is the condition of my interacting with other people. As we have seen, my body is always perspectival – I never have an all-encompassing hold on the world; there is therefore room for other incarnate subjectivities, and their points of view complement my own. Their body expresses their intentions and I perceive those intentions with my own body; insofar as my body takes up the other's intentions, there is an internal relation between our bodies. It is thus first of all the body which opens itself to others and responds to them; there is a mutual presence of incarnate subjects which precedes any alienation. The hold on the world which others have – and which they are – enriches me by enabling me to achieve a more comprehensive view of the world than is offered by my own hold alone. Far from being mutually exclusive, these multiple modes of being-in-the-world are internally related and form a social world. Just as in the perception of objects our perspectives 'slip into' each other and are brought together in the thing, so my perspective and that of other people 'slip into' each other and are brought together in a shared social world. Like the natural world, the social world is not 'a sum of objects' but a 'permanent field' with which we are in contact by the simple fact of existing, prior to any objectification or judgement about it. Merleau-Ponty points out that although I can turn away from the social world, I cannot 'cease to be situated relatively to it'. We already have an internal relation to the natural world in virtue of our possessing sensory functions and, as we have seen, it is impossible to sever the natural and the social, or to declare the one a 'lower layer'. The ambiguity which characterizes the phenomenal body therefore also pervades the social world; however, this ambiguity is not a defect to be deplored, since it is the very condition of our being human at all. Like the thing, the interworld lends itself to unending exploration, unending articulations, and ever fresh discoveries. Nonetheless, like the thing and the natural world, others and the human world are the very stuff of that pre-logical certainty which Merleau-Ponty will describe more fully in the next chapter.

Notes
1. It should be noted that modern philosophers have approached 'the problem of other minds' from various angles and have developed several different arguments to refute solipsism. For a discussion of the argument from analogy, behaviourism, the two-meanings view, the expression theory, the criteriological view, and the identity theory, see for example *The Philosophy of Mind*, V. C. Chappell (ed.), (Englewood Cliffs, N.J.: Prentice-Hall Inc., 1962).
2. Sartre, 'Concrete Relations With Others', *Being and Nothingness: a Phenomenological Essay on Ontology*, pp. 534–59.
3. Admittedly, there are passages in *Being and Nothingness* in which Sartre seems to go beyond such a Cartesian dualism to a view of incarnate consciousness more like that which Merleau-Ponty sub-

sequently developed in the *Phenomenology of Perception*. In this connection, one might mention Sartre's own criticism of Cartesian dualism (for example, see 'Introduction: The Pursuit of Being', pp. 3ff) as well as parts of his discussion of 'The Body', such as: 'Being-for-itself must be wholly body and it must be wholly consciousness; it can not be *united* with a body . . . '(p. 404); 'We know that there is not a for-itself on the one hand and a world on the other as two closed entities . . . ' (p. 405); 'The point of view of pure knowledge is contradictory; there is only the point of view of engaged knowledge . . . ' (p. 407); 'The body is nothing other than the for-itself . . . an engaged contingent being among other contingent beings . . . for the for-itself, to exist and to be situated are one and the same . . . ' (p. 408); ' . . . the very nature of the for-itself demands that it be body . . . ' (p. 409); 'My body is co-existive with the world, spread across all things, and at the same time it is condensed into this single point which I am without being able to know it . . . ' (p. 420); 'The body is *lived* and not known.' (p. 427); ' . . . glasses, pince-nez, monocles, *etc.*, which become, so to speak, a supplementary sense organ' (p. 433); 'The body is the totality of meaningful relations to the world' (p. 452); 'Thus my perception of the Other's body is radically different from my perception of things' (p. 453). 'These frowns, this redness, this stammering . . . these do not *express* anger; they *are* anger . . . . Thus it is not necessary to resort to habit or reason by analogy in order to explain how we *understand* expressive conduct. This conduct is originally released to perception as understandable; its meaning is part of its being just as the color of the paper is part of the being of the paper' (p. 455).

Yet despite these and similar passages, Sartre's position remains fundamentally dualistic and thus lacks that 'third term' which forms the nucleus of Merleau-Ponty's entire philosophy. It seems to me that the latter is essentially correct in his assessment when he declares that Sartre is 'a good Cartesian'; that 'in Sartre there is a plurality of subjects but no intersubjectivity'; that 'the apparent paradox of his work is that he became famous by describing a middle ground . . . between consciousness and things – the root in *Nausea*, viscosity or situation in *Being and Nothingness* . . . – and that nonetheless his thought is in revolt against this middle ground and finds there only an incentive to transcend it'; that 'contrary to appearances, being-for-itself is all Sartre has ever accepted, with its inevitable correlate: pure being-in-itself . . . . there is no hinge, no joint or mediation, between myself and the other'; that 'there is an encounter rather than a common action because, for Sartre, the social remains the relationship of "two individual consciousnesses" which look at each other'; that 'commitment in Sartre's sense is the negation of the link between us and the world that it seems to assert; or rather [that] Sartre tries to make a link out of a negation'; and that if, unlike Sartre, one recognizes a genuine 'interworld', then it is no longer a question of 'either him or me,' or an 'alternative of solipsism, or pure abnegation', because the relation-

ships 'in private [and] in public history . . . are no longer the
encounter of two For-Itselfs but are the meshing of two experiences
which, without ever coinciding, belong to a single world.' Merleau-
Ponty, *Adventures of the Dialectic*, Joseph Bien (trans.), (Evanston,
Ill: Northwestern University Press, 1973) pp. 147, 158–9; 205, 137,
142, 152, 193, 200.

4.   Sartre, 'The Body', *Being and Nothingness*, pp. 445–7.

Part III

Being-for-Itself and Being-in-the-World

1

The Cogito

As we enter the final part of the *Phenomenology*, it is useful to recall briefly the major points of Merleau-Ponty's phenomenological description so far. Already in the 'Preface', we learned that Merleau-Ponty's basic endeavour in this work is to awaken us to an awareness of our existence as incarnate subjects inhering in the world. Reflection on our lived experience revealed that the body itself is not a system of externally related parts but rather, that it is a dynamic synthesis of mutually implicatory powers. As a comprehensive project of such internally related powers, the body itself already outlines the fundamental features of the world in which these powers continually find their realization. Neither the body nor the world towards which the former is a transcendence, can be comprehended in isolation. The body is only a body in so far as it is this transcendence towards a world and by the same token, the world is only a world insofar as it is this polarization of bodily powers. Nonetheless, neither term is reducible to the other, because transcendence – as surpassing *towards* – implies objectivity, while objectivity comes into being only for a subject polarized towards it, and that subject is most immediately the body as a 'natural self '. There is thus an internal relationship between the body and the world; and it is within this relationship that all meaning emerges. Things are real when the body-subject has a hold on them as intersensory objects; and that inevitably involves a measure of ambiguity and incompleteness. Further, there is a genesis not only of objectivity, but also of subjectivity; and both poles of this body–world dialectic manifest a resistance to absorption which renders them relatively (but never absolutely) independent.

    The genesis of meaning was most directly shown to us in the chapter 'The Body as Expression and Speech', where we saw that the body-subject as a speaking subject finds itself already situated in a language which, as vehicle of sedimented meanings, can be used to bring into being a new meaning. To speak of language is of course to enter the realm of co-existence and culture. Merleau-Ponty followed up his preliminary discussion of this realm with a more detailed description of the way in which not only things and the natural world, but also others and the human world come into being for the incarnate subject. It emerged that insofar as things are apprehended within an already human context, the natural and the cultural orders merge into one another and are ultimately inseparable. It would seem then that there is no need to discuss the *cogito* – since the natural and the human world has been described, there would seem to be nothing further to say. Why does Merleau-Ponty nevertheless find it necessary to provide a discussion of the *cogito*? Is he simply so to speak 'paying his dues' to the tradition which he has been criticizing throughout this work? I think not; on the contrary, it seems to me that the chapter on the *cogito* is absolutely crucial in establishing the philosophical status of Merleau-Ponty's phenomenological description.

Up to this point, readers of the *Phenomenology* might well think that they can accept Merleau-Ponty's description of the body as the 'third term' lying between the extremes of mechanistic physiology and intellectualist psychology. They might be prepared to agree with Merleau-Ponty that there is a bodily synthesis in which the parts of our body are given to us immediately as already oriented towards the performance of tasks and the perception of things in the world. Further, readers might acknowledge that there is a bodily spatiality of the sort described by Merleau-Ponty and that our perception of things has to do with internal and external horizons which rule out absolutely exhaustive or unambiguous perceptions. Finally, readers might be prepared to admit that our perception of others is characterized by the same opacity and ambiguity; that our gestures and our speech are neither constructed nor simply 'triggered off ' and that our dialogue with others is not to be understood as the translating and decoding of ready- made thoughts. All this, then, may be conceded; however, readers may argue that the description so far really belongs to the domain of psychology and sociology – that it deals merely with the manner in which we live our daily lives, our way of relating to things, to our cultural heritage, and to others with whom we come into contact in our daily affairs.

It may be said that of course we do not preface our actions, our perceptions, or our conversations with reflections concerning the position of our limbs and the location of objects, or the signifi-

cance of the words we are about to utter. It is perfectly obvious
that for the most part we carry on our lives at a pre-reflective level.
But does not all this merely underline – so it may be argued – the
radical distinction between lived experience and reflection? Does
it not emphasize the peculiar nature and task of a genuine
philosophy? Our daily life, our personal existence might well be
fraught with ambiguity, uncertainty and obscurity; fortunately
however, in doing philosophy we can transcend these elements
and enter the realm of pure reflection. It is precisely the task of
philosophy to clarify, to dispel uncertainty and ambiguity. Although we do not in our daily exchanges with others translate
ready-made thoughts into speech, this in no way indicates – so it
may be pointed out – that we *cannot* take refuge in a domain of
pure thought. In fact, it is precisely our failure to do this which
renders our pre-reflective life opaque and ambiguous. However, if
we pause to engage in reflection, we enter a realm of consciousness in which we can attain the kind of clarity essential to
certainty and truth; and this is surely the domain of any philosophy worthy of the name. The present chapter on the *cogito*
addresses exactly these sorts of concerns, which readers of the
Phenomenology might well have at this point. The very attempt to
establish a realm of pure thought as indubitable ground of all
knowledge or truth is therefore now submitted to investigation.
The underlying question is whether there can in fact *be* such a
realm of pure ideas, of thoughts lacking all temporality or contingency; whether there can be an absolute interiority in which
consciousness is utterly transparent to itself so that nothing eludes
its grasp.

Like Descartes, Merleau-Ponty begins the investigation with
perception and the recognition that 'our senses sometimes deceive
us'. Nonetheless, despite the fact that what I take to be an ash-try
may turn out on closer inspection to be a paperweight or even just
a shadow cast on the table by the sunlight filtering into the room,
it would seem that my act of perception itself – unlike its object –
is absolutely indubitable. Surely I cannot be mistaken in *thinking*
that I see an ash-tray; surely I can be in error only insofar as I
assert the actual existence of the ash-tray. Steeped as we are in the
Cartesian tradition of detaching the subject from the object, we
generally consider such a separating of perception from the
percept to pose no problem. However, at the conclusion of the
chapter 'The Body as Expression and Speech', Merleau-Ponty

explicitly cautioned us against adopting this approach. We saw that the body itself is not an object, nor our awareness of it an idea; moreover, we discovered that the ambiguity inherent in the body's mode of existence is not restricted to the body itself but 'spreads to the perceived world in its entirety'. Not only the body, but things and other people come into being for us; and our awareness of them is ultimately inseparable from that anonymous dynamic interaction with the world which we find at the level of pre-reflective life. In submitting the perceived world to a truly radical reflection, we found that the object of perception is not a ready-made existence but rather, one pole of a pre-personal bodily experience; and hence, that the traditional distinction between the object's appearance and its reality is fundamentally wrong-headed. In making explicit the theory of perception which is already implicit in the phenomenological theory of the body image, the previous chapters have made it clear that perception cannot be divorced from its object, because the very structure of the act already implies the existence of that towards which it is polarized. The Cartesian position which dissociates the actual existence of the thing seen from our consciousness of seeing it, is therefore untenable. As Merleau-Ponty points out, 'if I see an ash-tray, *in the full sense of the word see*, there must be an ash-tray there'.

At this stage it might be retorted that perception does not lead us into the realm of pure thought because perception is a peculiar sort of activity; and that we must therefore adopt a different point of departure for our voyage into the interior realm. Perception – so it may be argued – inherently involves the risk of error because it has to do with figure–background structures, with perspectives which cannot all be given simultaneously. It is after all easy enough to see that our perception of a table, for example, always has to do with a certain angle of the table – I see the top of it while the bottom is hidden from me, or vice versa. Consequently, there is a built-in uncertainty about perception which – so it may be claimed – inevitably renders our thought about perception dubitable too. We therefore turn from perception bearing on objects in the world, to perception having to do exclusively with our own psychic states – we turn from 'outer' to 'inner' perception. Here, surely, consciousness will be completely transparent to itself and there will be no possibility of error. Our awareness of our psychic states will surely coincide with their actual existence; we cannot after all be deceived regarding our own feelings – to feel sad is to be sad and to love is to be conscious of loving. We might thus argue that the circuit of our own subjectivity constitutes a sphere of absolute certainty.

As Merleau-Ponty shows, however, this is not the case; we do in fact distinguish between 'true' and 'false' emotions. Love, for example, can be mistaken or illusory; hence, far from being transparent to itself, it is profoundly ambiguous. This ambiguity is even more apparent in cases of hysteria: to maintain that the patient is deliberately making an error with respect to his own emotions or that he is feigning them, is to misconstrue his experience; but on the other hand, the patient readily recognizes the difference between the terror he feels when confronted with a real weapon, and that which he feels in face of the insubstantial dagger called up by his hallucinations. Though tempting, it is useless to invoke an unconscious here, as Merleau-Ponty points out.[1] Like external perception, internal perception is always incomplete, always open-ended, because it also is a transcendence of the human being towards the world. Our emotions cannot be isolated from the world; the consciousness of loving is the consciousness which we have of situating ourselves in the world in a particular way. Our contact with our emotions is therefore always 'achieved only in the sphere of ambiguity'.

If even our 'inner states' are thus open to illusions, does not illusion itself become a meaningless term? How are we ever to describe any of our psychic states as authentic in the absence of any invariable criterion or measuring rod, any absolute truth against which our 'inner' and 'outer' perceptions can be judged to be genuine or illusory? In short, do we not condemn ourselves to endless doubt if we accept this analysis of inner and outer perceptions? In an effort to avoid such a situation, we may turn to the understanding in a final attempt to achieve the absolute self-coincidence of thought. The understanding after all deals with the sorts of proofs and truths which would seem to preclude the opacity and ambiguity encountered so far. Merleau-Ponty therefore examines the kind of truths with which geometry deals, and reveals that the geometer's thought does not in fact coincide with itself. The geometer's thinking never manages to transcend perceptual consciousness altogether, because it is ultimately based on the geometer's experience of real triangles. The truths of geometry are rooted in the spatiality and motility of the geometer's own body.

The truths of geometry are therefore sustained by the original intentionality of the body; they are in fact expressions based on the body-subject as primordially expressive. The geometer already operates within a universe of discourse which he takes for granted. His truths are not pure self-sustaining thoughts but rather, cultural objects which are necessarily linked to concrete acts of expression. Merleau-Ponty consequently turns to a re-examination of language and of the relationship between thought and speech. This examination reveals that there is in fact no pure transcendent thought behind language but rather, that 'language transcends itself in speech'. Expression is inherently temporal and always retains 'its coefficient of facticity'. No analysis can rid language of its fundamental obscurity; the search for a realm of pure thought, of absolute eternal truth, has turned out to be a doomed effort. Every thought about thought has shown itself to be ultimately rooted in perceptual consciousness, thereby leaving us with 'a temporal thickness', with a contingency which cannot be conjured away. Nonetheless, what has to be realized is that this obscurity, this ambiguity, is not the index of any defect or deficiency but rather, that it is the very condition of our access to knowledge, self-evidence, certainty and truth. There is, finally, no realm of self-sustaining thought, no realm of 'pure reflection' in the traditional sense, to which philosophy could withdraw. And yet, our external and internal perceptions are self-affirming; 'there are truths, just as there are perceptions'. It is up to the philosopher to bring to our awareness our fundamental 'being-in-truth', to reveal the realm of discourse upon which the spoken *cogito* draws and to point to the unspoken – or tacit – *cogito* which forms its primordial background.

Let us consider the *cogito* itself in more detail. The *cogito* is first of all a thought formed at a particular time in a particular place by a particular philosopher – Descartes – who was himself situated in a particular cultural order and thinking within a particular philosophical tradition. That thought, embodied in Descartes' writings, itself became part of the cultural–philosophical acquisition of subsequent thinkers – such as Merleau-Ponty. The *cogito* is therefore 'a cultural being' which can be taken up and rethought; and our own thought, in reaching out to it, thereby itself re-enacts

Realism → things + ideas exist in themselves. Truth is transcendent (in the world) and beyond man's complete understanding

the *cogito* and can subsequently submit its own act to reflection. Descartes believed the *cogito* to be eternally true; in reflecting on his *cogito* and our own via Merleau-Ponty's phenomenological description we will consequently need to reconsider the nature of truth. We have seen that the 'natural attitude to things' makes us oblivious of the incarnate subject's contribution to the perceived world; moreover, we have seen that realism goes on to claim that things and ideas exist in themselves. In calling for a return to the subject, the Cartesian *cogito* thus embodies a valid insight. Our experience of things as transcendent individual objects and our recognition of ideas as ideas, require that we project ourselves towards them in a certain way; their existence for us as things and ideas respectively, depends upon our actualizing our primordial power of knowing them as such. Their existence as transcendent beings implies, however, that we do not know them exhaustively and will never acquire an all-encompassing grasp of them. This inherent measure of ignorance in our awareness of things and ideas raises the Socratic problem of how we can simultaneously know something sufficiently to seek it and to recognize it when we encounter it, yet not know it, so as to prompt us to seek it. The phenomenological response to this classic problem consists in showing – as Merleau-Ponty has done in the previous chapters – that our relationship to the world and to ourselves is not an 'all or nothing' affair; neither do we simply invent things by endowing them with whatever we subsequently ascribe to them, nor do we run up against them as entities existing entirely in themselves which we merely observe. Our perception and reasoning are neither blind nor transparent; instead, as we have seen, there is a knowing which lies between the traditional extremes of realism on the one hand and idealism on the other. Its partial validity notwithstanding, the Cartesian return to the self misses this third kind of knowing and its positing of clear and distinct ideas, or 'eternal essences', existing in a translucent, timeless mind – the thinking ego. The latter's absolute self-possession rules out receptivity as well as any sort of inherence in the world – including even its own personal history. Thus the Cartesian consciousness is ultimately God; moreover, its absolute thought precludes the existence of any other consciousness, thereby condemning it to a solipsistic existence.

We saw in the last chapter why 'the constituting consciousness is necessarily unique and universal' and why a philosophy which

[margin note: Meno's Paradox]

idealism → ideas : eternal essences, existing in a translucent, timeless mind (the thinking ego). Truth is immanent in the mind & ultimately God affirms the existence of such a consciousness falls into irresolvable difficulties. We must therefore resolutely abandon this absolute *cogito* which ejects us from the world, blocks intersubjectivity and destroys temporality; instead, we must pursue the phenomenological description of our relationship with things, others, ideas and ourselves, so as to arrive at a *cogito* compatible with our lived experience. In short, we must elaborate the nature of that 'hold' on the world and on ourselves which makes our experience possible while preventing its ever becoming completely transparent for us.

Earlier, we saw that our perception by its very nature adheres to the world, and that Descartes was fundamentally misguided in attempting to sever the two terms by transforming perception into an indubitable thought while declaring the actual existence of the perceived world to be uncertain.[2] The previous chapters showed us that perception is not a third person process or psychic fact occurring in us, and that our consciousness of perception is not a 'passive noting' of a self-contained event. Nor is the awareness of perception pure construction by an all-inclusive constituting consciousness; rather, we have seen that perception is the transcending of a body-subject towards a world and that this action always involves an ambiguous self-awareness. The certainty of seeing or hearing is inseparable from that bodily project which *is* the act of seeing or the act of hearing; hence the phenomenological *cogito* – unlike its Cartesian counterpart – is the recognition of that primordial project of transcendence which is our very being.

Far from absorbing phenomena into private psychic states or declaring them the possession of a translucent thought, the phenomenological *cogito* discloses the indissolubility of the link between our being and that of the world; it affirms our pre-reflective 'hold' on ourselves as 'being-in-the-world'. The fact that we are primordially situated in the world precludes our ever enjoying the self-transparency of the Cartesian consciousness; instead, it renders our contact with ourselves and the world inherently ambiguous. The phrase 'being-in-the-world' expresses an existential relationship having an existential significance, rather than a mental or mechanical relation having a purely intellectual or mechanistic meaning. Consequently, our own emotions, for example, are neither drives concealed from us in an unconscious realm, nor objects spread out for a disinterested mental viewing. On the contrary, our emotions are lived ambiguously as an inextricable part of our pre-reflective 'relationship with the world'; they are neither noted nor constituted, but experienced. The phenomenological *cogito* thus recognizes 'a middle course' lying between unconscious drives or representations on the one hand, and pure ideas or explicit knowledge on the other.

The middle course which phenomenology takes describes human existence as 'action or doing' – and hence, as perpetual self-transcending. On the phenomenological view, we therefore neither elude nor possess ourselves completely. In *Being and Nothingness* Sartre shows that there must be a non-positional self-consciousness anterior to the Cartesian *cogito*:

> If we wish to avoid an infinite regress, there must be an immediate, non-cognitive relation of the self to itself. . . . The immediate consciousness which I have of perceiving . . . . does not *know* my perception, does not *posit* it; all that there is of intention in my actual consciousness is directed toward the outside, toward the world. In turn, this spontaneous consciousness of my perception is *constitutive* of my perceptive consciousness. . . . Thus reflection has no kind of primacy over the consciousness reflected-on. It is not reflection which reveals the consciousness reflected-on to itself. Quite the contrary, it is the non-reflective consciousness which renders the reflection possible; there is a pre-reflective cogito which is the condition of the Cartesian cogito.[3]

Without actually referring to *Being and Nothingness*, Merleau-Ponty follows the Sartrian position here in elaborating the meaning of existence as action. Mere thoughts about thinking, doubting, perceiving or feeling do not as such establish our certainty of existing; rather, the certainty of our thoughts rests on that of our actions. Our knowledge of ourselves is inherently mediated by our relationship to the world; hence 'inner perception' is not self-sustaining, but depends upon our actually involving ourselves in experiences such as seeing something or doubting something or loving someone. In the absence of such actual performance, or 'doing', our own existence would be entirely insubstantial, or 'unreal' – or rather, we would not even exist because, as Sartre points out, 'what is truly unthinkable is passive existence'.[4]

In order to make ourselves the object of our thought, we must first of all exist as being-in-the-world; moreover, the act of objectification itself escapes objectification – we can never, so to speak, 'catch ourselves by the tail'. Underlying any thetic knowledge of ourselves or the world is that pre-reflective anonymous existence of a body-subject polarized by a world, which earlier chapters of the *Phenomenology* have described. As Merleau-Ponty stressed in the chapter 'The Theory of the Body is Already a Theory of Perception', 'we are our body . . . by thus remaking contact with the body and with the world, we shall also rediscover ourself . . .'. We have seen that the pre-personal subject–world dialogue brings about the synthesis of things through the pre-reflective synthesis of the body itself; that these syntheses are mutually implicatory; that neither synthesis is ever exhaustive. Primordial experience is thus inherently open-ended – but that does not render it uncertain; like 'external perception', our 'internal perception' is simultaneously incomplete and self-affirming.

Our perception of the world and of ourselves is fraught with ambiguity; yet not only are we open to illusion and to truth about the world and about ourselves, but we can and do distinguish truth from illusion in both cases by the kind of 'hold' which we have on the respective phenomena. It is this which the phenomenological *cogito* recognizes and affirms. Far from reducing existence to thought about existence, this *cogito* reintegrates thought into the total project which is our existence as being-in-the-world. As Merleau-Ponty points out at the conclusion of his chapter 'Sensing', 'reflection does not itself grasp its full meaning ['sens'] unless it refers to the unreflective fund of experience which it presupposes, upon which it draws, and which constitutes for it a kind of original past'. The *cognito* recognizes that our fundamental inherence in the world is the source of all certainty; interpreted in this way, the *cogito* is at the very core of that truly radical reflection which simultaneously restores thought to the incarnate subject and the incarnate subject to the world.

The *cogito* of the Cartesian philosophy is bound up with Descartes' claims that we really perceive only with our intellect, that 'for a perception to be a possible foundation for a certain and indubitable judgment, it must be not only clear but also distinct', that whatever we 'clearly and distinctly perceive is necessarily true' and that the entire foundation for 'the certainty and truth of all knowledge' is our 'awareness of the true God'.[5] Merleau-Ponty's phenomenological description has called these claims into question; consequently, it is encumbent on Merleau-Ponty to provide an alternative conception of truth for his *cogito*, and he does so in discussing Descartes' example of a triangle. In his Fifth Meditation Descartes argues that

> when I imagine a triangle, it may be that no such figure exists anywhere outside my consciousness (*cogitationem*), or never has existed; but there certainly exists its determinate nature (its essence, its form), which is unchangeable and eternal. This is no figment of mine, and does not depend on my mind, as is clear from the following: various properties can be proved of this triangle. . . . All these properties are true, since I perceive them clearly . . .[6]

We saw earlier that this attempt to sever ideas from our being-in-the-world is fundamentally flawed; hence there cannot be a 'formal essence' or 'pure idea' of a triangle. In fact, its retrospective nature proves that formal thought is based on intuitive thought and it is at the level of the latter that all our certainty and truth emerge. In the absence of any concrete experience of things and *de facto* truth, we would be unable even to formulate mathematical or scientific hypotheses and to formalize relations in definitions. The essence of the triangle formalizes a particular way of relating ourselves to the world and is therefore dynamic; moreover, it is implied in our general 'hold on the world' and presupposes that space which is brought into being by the primordial motility of the body-subject. The thought of the geometer is part of a cultural world which is based on the incarnate subject's pre-personal transcendence towards a pre-objective world. As we have seen, this transcendence is of its very nature ongoing, open-ended, incomplete and ambiguous because it is synonymous with our very existence itself. The apparent clarity and completion of the geometer's triangle is predicated on the tacit assumption that the physical triangle of perceptual consciousness can be completely synthesized; and this assumption of course involves the concomitant assumption that the synthesis of the body itself can be completed. Like any other type of thinking, mathematics is historically and geographically situated and in nowise expresses eternal truths. The properties which Descartes declares necessarily true of all triangles, in fact characterize only those belonging to a certain type of space – as the advent of non-Euclidean geometry showed.

Our ability to modulate our hold on the world renders Euclidean space contingent and makes other types of space possible. Within the framework of a particular view of the world, various truths will strike us as being self-evident; however, even these truths are never unchallengeable – as we discover when we change our hold on the world and thereby transform the 'ground' for our thoughts. Because being-in-the-world means being situated – and thus being perspectival without ever being sealed into any single perspective – certainty is inherently conditional. To protest that such certainty is no certainty at all, is to misunderstand the nature of certainty and to forget Merleau-Ponty's admonition that we must revise our usual notions of contingency and necessity. It is, moreover to neglect or dismiss the phenomenological critique of Cartesian thinking.

As we saw above, only an absolute consciousness could have an unchallengeable certainty; but such a non-perspectival consciousness would be unsituated and thus, non-human. In fact, it would be no consciousness at all because, lacking any transcendence, it would collapse and cease to exist (as Sartre's detailed arguments in the *The Transcendence of the Ego* and *Being and Nothingness* demonstrate). There is neither a disembodied consciousness nor a domain of absolute truth; since we inhere in the world and in time, our truths always retain their element of facticity – they are the truths of a perspectival, temporal being and like the latter, they are essentially dynamic and open-ended. Contrary to our common conception of the matter, it is therefore ultimately impossible to distinguish between 'truths of fact' and 'truths of reason'; their relationship is one of *Fundierung*. In virtue of existing as a fundamental project, we always already 'take up' truths of fact; and in carrying them forward and making them explicit, we transform them into truths of reason without thereby severing them from our being-in-the-world. Truths of reason become sedimented into the cultural tradition and thus in turn become part of the presupposed foundation for our thoughts. In being born into a natural and cultural world, we are consequently born into a participation in truth; moreover, just as it is impossible to free ourselves from any 'inherence in the world', so it is impossible to survey or to 'bracket' all our presuppositions so as to attain Husserl's dream of an absolute (presuppositionless) evidence. Absolute knowledge is forever precluded because our experience of truth is inseparable from our being in a situation; however, absolute falsity is ruled out by the same token. The phenomenological conception of truth goes beyond both dogmatism and scepticism by showing that ' "being-in-truth" is indistinguishable from being-in-the-world'.

To say that truth is never unconditional, is not to reduce it to being merely the effect of our own particular psycho-physiological makeup. Nor is it to divorce the phenomenon from being and to declare the latter inaccessible to us. For phenomenology, the phenomenon is not 'mere appearance', because being *is* 'that which appears'; moreover, the appearing of being is inseparable from the being to which it appears – that is, from incarnate consciousness. Once again, it is a matter of recognizing the primordial dialogue in which things, other people and the natural and cultural world as a whole, begin to exist for us prior to any reflection. There is no ontological – nor logical – necessity governing this pre-reflective genesis of being on which all our thoughts (including our ideas of truth) are based. And yet, this does not mean our thought, our self-evident truth is merely 'one fact among others'; rather, it is 'a value-fact which envelops and conditions every other possible one'. Necessity and possibility are themselves based on the primordial fact of our existing as perceiving, thinking beings. No matter how we may doubt or err, our basic hold on the world ensures that we remain open to certainty and truth for the entire duration of our existence; moreover, our errors and illusions, when recognized as such, become truths and contribute to the never-ending process of forging ever more complete truths. Whereas the Cartesian *cogito* purports to put us into direct contact with an intelligible realm of truths in themselves, while neglecting even to mention that concrete world of discourse which sustains and conditions it from start to finish, the phenomenological reflection draws our attention not only to Descartes' 'spoken *cogito*', but also to that 'silent *cogito*' from which it springs. Radical reflection recognizes that its thinking is inextricably embodied in a language and rooted in a history. It reminds us, in reflecting on the Cartesian *cogito*, that explicit subjectivity and thinking about thought presuppose an 'indeclinable subjectivity' which is synonymous with our very being-in-the-world. Prior to any philosophizing, there is that comprehensive, pre-personal experience in which the body-subject comes into being by simultaneously grasping the world and itself. This purely generalized, pre-reflective *cogito* is the foundation of all our truths; and a genuinely radical reflection sets itself the task of bringing it to our awareness.

Notes

1. For a fuller discussion, see also Sartre's *The Emotions: Outline of a Theory*, Bernard Frechtman (trans.), (New York: Philosophical Library, 1948). The French original predates Merleau-Ponty's *Phenomenology of Perception*, and the latter's view of the emotions is in many respects analogous to that presented by Sartre.

2. At the conclusion of his 'Second Meditation' Descartes states: 'I now know that even bodies are not really perceived by the senses or the imaginative faculty, but only by the intellect; that they are perceived, not by being touched or seen, but by being understood; I thus clearly recognize that nothing is more easily or manifestly perceptible to me than my own mind.' In the 'Third Meditation' Descartes adds: 'Now ideas considered in themselves, and not referred to something else, cannot strictly speaking be false. . . . Only judgments remain; it is here that I must take precaution against falsehood. Now the chief and commonest error that is to be found in this field consists in my taking ideas within myself to have similarity or conformity to some external object . . .'. In the 'Fourth Meditation' Descartes says: 'Now when I do not perceive clearly and distinctly enough what the truth is, it is clear that if I abstain from judgment I do right and am not deceived.' In the 'Fifth Meditation' Descartes summarizes his 'criterion of truth': 'But now I have discerned that God exists, and have understood at the same time that everything else depends on him, and that he is not deceitful; and from this I have gathered that whatever I clearly and distinctly perceive is necessarily true.' (*Philosophical Writings*, Anscombe and Geach (trans. and eds) pp. 75, 78, 98, 107.). Finally, it is worth noting that in his *Principles of Philosophy* Descartes says: '[The mind] finds within itself ideas of many things; and so long as it merely contemplates these, and neither asserts nor denies the existence of something like them outside itself, it cannot be in error.' (Ibid., p. 184).

3. Sartre, *Being and Nothingness: A Phenomenological Essay on Ontology*, pp. 12–13. See also Sartre's *The Transcendence of the Ego: an Existentialist Theory of Consciousness*.

4. Ibid., p. 16.

5. Descartes, *Philosophical Writings*, pp. 75, 190, 107, 108.

6. Ibid., p. 102.

2

Temporality

Common sense divorces the world from the subject and the latter's thought from its body. In proceeding from the body and the perceived world to the *cogito*, our investigation has overturned this division and juxtaposition of the 'external' and 'internal' by showing them to be inseparable. We have seen that subjectivity cannot be detached from the body itself; that the latter, as a primordial project, is inextricably tied to the perceived world; and finally, that thought itself is never 'pure' but rather, presupposes perceptual consciousness and remains inseverable from it. Thought, subjectivity, body and world are therefore mutually implicatory; they form a single comprehensive system in which each term can be equally designated as 'inside' or 'outside' – hence Merleau-Ponty was able to declare at the conclusion of the last chapter that 'the world is wholly inside and I am wholly outside myself '. In reflecting on the being of each aspect of the subject–world system, we have already encountered temporality at various points because perception, being inherently perspectival, is of its very nature temporal. Perception moreover requires the synthesis of the body itself; and this synthesis involves a spatiality and motility whose existence implies that of time. We have seen that the perceived world comes into being for a bodily transcendence; and it would be a contradiction in terms to declare transendence non-temporal. Thus temporality has been implicit in Merleau-Ponty's entire phenomenological description of perception; however, the being of time must now be examined explicitly so that we may achieve a better understanding of the subjectivity which the *cogito* revealed. In addition, the analysis of time will enable us to resolve the problems raised by objective thought regarding the relation of body to soul and self to others, as well as the question of what the world was like prior to the emergence of humans.

The common conception of time likens it to the flowing of a river – a metaphor whose frequent use has led us generally to accept its applicability without realizing its confusion. Flowing implies change of place – for example, the river flows from its source in the mountains down into the sea – but change implies a situated observer without whom there can be no 'down' or 'from' or 'to' and, in short, no flow. Not only is there no flowing river existing in-itself, but its alleged temporal sequence is also profoundly misleading. Whereas the metaphor assumes that the river flows out of the past towards the future, the tacit introduction of the necessary observer reverses the temporal sequence. As Merleau-Ponty points out, the water passing the observer surreptitiously stationed on the riverbank, is not pushed towards the future but rather, sinks into the past. Similarly, for the observer tacitly assumed to be swept along by the current, the landscapes lying ahead are the future and the course of time is not the river itself but rather, the landscape rolling by. Since it presupposes a perspective, time is neither 'a flowing substance' nor a third person process to be recorded; on the contrary, time comes into being from our relationship to the world and has no existence apart from that relation. Further, since subjectivity *is* the act of transcendence towards a world which thereby comes into being as world, we can say that we ourselves are time. Radical reflection thus brings us to a view of time which is the opposite of that suggested by the river metaphor; nonetheless, the analogy is justified in so far as it precludes breaking time into a succession of discrete moments or reducing it to a juxtaposition of objective positions which we occupy in turn. In comparing it to a fountain in which there is a single thrust of water instead of a series of separate waves, common sense recognizes the essential unity of time. Unfortunately however, it undermines this insight by objectifying time – which is not to say, of course, that the Kantian approach is any more valid in positing time as a pure form. Once again, both realism and idealism must be abandoned if we are to understand the phenomenon – in this case, that of time.

Ironically, common sense congeals time in making it into a being comparable to a river or fountain existing in-itself. Thus it suggests that the water which will soon flow by is now making its way down the mountain, for example, while that which has just flowed past is presently further downstream. It is not a matter here of collapsing time by arguing – as is frequently done – that neither the past nor the future actually exists and that the present, strictly defined, is absolutely instantaneous and hence, being

totally without extension, likewise is non-existent. On the contrary, by making the future pre-exist, the present exist and the past
survive, the common sense view renders them all present in the
objective world so that, conceived as existing in-itself, the world is
completely full of 'instances of "now" '. Common sense of course
implies that the latter form a sequence; however, there can in fact
be neither a 'now' nor a sequence once the subject has been
removed. The notion of a present which is not present to anyone,
is profoundly inconsistent – as is that of a succession which
occurs in the absence of any subject. Being-in-itself is utter
plenitude; and since future and past require non-being, the
objective world effectively excludes time. By divorcing it from
subjectivity, common sense loses any possibility of introducing
nothingness into the world; hence it cannot sustain temporal
dimensions and is left with the solidity of being which simply *is*
what it is.

In his criticism of objective thought, Merleau-Ponty here bases
himself on Sartre's detailed phenomenological analysis of being-
in-itself, nothingness and temporality – an analysis which, in
turn, owes much to the works of Husserl and Heidegger.[1] In *Being
and Nothingness* Sartre states that we cannot comprehend being-
in-the-world by breaking this synthetic relation apart or reducing it
to either of its terms. He argues that being-in-itself is solid
plenitude which on principle forbids becoming and 'is not subject
to temporality'. He shows that nothingness comes into the world
through the human being and that the latter's very being must be
temporality. Sartre argues that temporality is neither a contingent
quality of consciousness nor a summation of instants; and that any
attempt to break time into static elements is doomed to fail. He
shows that the temporal dimensions are internally related; that the
for-itself temporalizes itself by existing as a project and that it
must simultaneously exist in all its dimensions. Transcendence, or
surpassing, implies that which is being surpassed and that towards which the project is surpassing: the former is the past and
the latter is the future; moreover, the past and future are always
those of a certain present. Sartre goes on to argue that reducing the
past to a collection of present memories not only presupposes 'the
being of the past', but also precludes our comprehending the
'pastness' of the past – its 'being back there'. Similarly, divorcing
the past from the present deprives the former of its 'pastness' and,
by turning it into a thing, once again destroys time. Past, present

and future can neither be reduced to, nor severed from, one another; they are inextricably related in that single upsurge of consciousness existing as being-in-the-world.

Tacitly taking up Sartre's argument, Merleau-Ponty elaborates the fallaciousness of attempting to account for our consciousness of pastness and futurity by recourse to the possession or projection of memories. It matters little whether such attempts are couched in physiological or in psychological terms (for example, 'engrams' or 'psychic traces'); both approaches offer no more than 'a simple factual presence' while presupposing a sense of the past and the future. In and of themselves, present data are totally incapable of opening a past or a future for us; they cannot prompt either recollection or anticipation in the absence of any direct contact with the temporal dimensions. In short, memory and projection presuppose precisely that which they are intended to explain. The being of past, present and future is not identical; none of the three dimensions can be 'explained' or constructed out of the others and none can exist without the others. As long as we insist on locating it in things themselves or in 'states of consciousness', we will misunderstand the being of time. Time is neither undergone nor constituted by us, because it is itself our living relationship with the world. Consequently, we can no more encompass time than we can circumscribe our own life; and by the same token, we can never be sealed into any single temporal dimension, but always exist as a living synthesis of all three.

How then are we to describe 'true time' – that primordial experience of time which underlies our notions of transience, duration and eternity? Merleau-Ponty suggests that it is in our 'field of presence' broadly speaking that we learn the interrelation of the temporal dimensions. When we remember an incident that happened some years ago, for example, we do not call up an idea or image of it; rather we 'reopen time' and carry ourselves back through the chain of intervening years to the time when it was part of our field of presence. As such, that field had its horizons of the future and the immediate past; but subsequently, of course, that future became present, the incident itself became part of an immediate past and what had been the immediate past become more remote. Then the future which had become present became in its turn the immediate past – and so on. In returning to the field of presence, we therefore see that the present and future are not pushed by the past as the river metaphor leads us to believe. On the contrary, we see in consulting our own experience that the future slides 'into the present and on into the past' and thus, that a formerly future horizon becomes closed and a formerly proximate past becomes ever more distant. None of the temporal dimensions is posited; rather, we experience the future as being ahead of us and the past as being behind us as we pursue our present task. The impending future weighs on us while the immediate past recedes from us with the arrival of each fresh present. The latter, moreover, not only brings about a transformation in its predecessor, but helps to determine the shape of its own successor.

Drawing on Husserl's *Phenomenology of Internal Time-Consciousness*, Merleau-Ponty emphasizes that intentionalities (Husserl's 'protentions' and 'retentions') connect us to the future and the past, thereby anchoring us to our environment. Far from being a line composed of discrete instants or preserved pictures of events, time is a network of overlapping intentionalities whose centre is none other than the body-subject itself as primordial intentionality. There is neither a mechanistic causality nor an intellectualist synthesis at work in the genesis of time, because time is quite simply the project which we ourselves are – that '*ek-stase*' of which Heidegger spoke in *Being and Time*. We temporalize ourselves by existing; hence there is no need for any explicit unification or synthesis of dimensions. As we have seen in earlier chapters, we have a pre-personal, pre-reflective 'hold' on the world and on ourselves; and in virtue of this primordial grip, we have a past and future whose existence requires no more verification than does that of the world or of ourselves. We are able to reach ahead to our future in anticipation or back to our past in recollection, because our present is not closed in upon itself; rather, it 'outruns itself ' in both directions. We do not keep the same hold on our past as it loses its immediacy and recedes below an ever increasing temporal thickness; nonetheless, we do not become totally severed from it either – it remains potentially retrievable. True temporality is not something which we conceive or observe; it is the process of living our lives and there is a sense in which our present is not only this moment or this week, but our entire life.

Primary temporality is a dynamic unity whose dimensions overlap one another without ever coinciding: the future is an impending present which will become past in due course; the present is 'an impending past and a recent future'; and 'the past is a former future and a recent present'. Time is therefore not a sequence of 'external events' or 'internal states' but rather, a chain of interlocking 'fields of presence'. If we are to avoid an infinite regress, we must recognize that there is an immediate, non-cognitive awareness of temporality – which should come as no surprise, since we have already seen that there is such a non-thetic consciousness of subjectivity and that time is the subject itself. Once again, our pre-reflective awareness is not unambiguous; just as the perspectivity of perceptual consciousness precludes our ever perceiving everything simultaneously, so that of our temporal consciousness rules out our ever having an all-encompassing grasp of time. There is thus no defect in our temporal perspective insofar as it gives us a present with its horizons, while preventing our simultaneously inhabiting other fields of presence. We have a hold on our past through a continuous chain of interlocked retentions, but we cannot juxtapose the links of that chain so as to grasp the whole of our past with equal clarity. Time synthesizes itself in that ceaseless sliding of the future into the present and on into the past, thereby giving us the illusion of eternity. Yet a timeless time is a contradiction in terms; and the unity of time is not something which comes about *in spite of* the temporal dimensions. Past, present and future compose an indivisible project; and to eliminate the distinctiveness of those dimensions would be to destroy the project – in short, to abolish time altogether.

This phenomenological description of temporality elucidates the nature of subjectivity, and helps us to resolve other problems encountered in our sustained criticism of objective thought. Merleau-Ponty's remarks regarding temporality and subjectivity are initially puzzling; and it is tempting to conclude that he is simply guilty of a rather glaring inconsistency in declaring both that the subject is to be 'identified with temporality' (likewise, that 'we must understand time as the subject and the subject as time') *and* that the subject is situated in time ('time exists for me only because I am situated in it'). Such an alleged inconsistency, however, arises only if we insist on retaining a traditional idea of time and of the subject – be it empirical or transcendental. Thus, if we conceive the subject as an essentially closed entity, provided that we do not accord it absolute status, we might consider it situated in time like a straw carried along by a river. Yet on such a view, we will find Merleau-Ponty's identification of subjectivity with temporality quite incomprehensible. If we conceive the subject as a constituting consciousness or transcendental ego, we *might* succeed in identifying it *very loosely* with time considered as a succession of states of consciousness. However, we will then find Merleau-Ponty's insistence on *situating* the subject *in* time to be very problematic because – as we have seen – such a Cartesian (or Kantian) subject is necessarily absolute and hence, cannot be situated. Merleau-Ponty's phenomenological account of the *cogito* and of temporality is precisely designed to make us relinquish these traditional conceptions.

As long as we cling to the transcendental ego, for example, we will render ourselves incapable of comprehending our actual experience. We have seen that such a thinking subject must be absolutely transparent and hence, that it cannot inhere in the world or have even a personal history. In an effort to account for our experience of positing or becoming aware of ourselves in time, we may supplement the constituting subject with an empirical self; but the latter, being an object constituted by the former, cannot in fact be a self. As soon as we put aside such a conception of subjectivity on the other hand, the contradiction in self-positing disappears. As Husserl's famous diagram shows, each fresh present transforms the entire temporal network. This ongoing transformation is not a matter of external causality, since the new present and the whole chain of preceding fields of presence are but a single comprehensive movement, which is the project of a life in process of unfolding. Self-positing is therefore of the essence of primordial temporality: time as a projecting ('thrust') affects itself as time already unfolded; and this 'dehiscence of the present towards a future' is subjectivity. The self is both affecting and affected – it is self-affecting, rather than unchanging self-identity. As Sartre shows in *Being and Nothingness*, there is an inherent duality at the heart of consciousness which is not to be confused with dualism.[2] Consequently, our reflection on time is itself situated in time; our reflection on subjectivity is itself part of our subjectivity. We can never coincide with ourselves – and yet we are present to ourselves precisely *because* we have the distance of non-coincidence. To make the subject into an ego which constitutes its experiences, is to eliminate that crucial distance and hence, to destroy conciousness.

Temporality not only establishes the essential non-coincidence of subjectivity, but by the same token, ensures its openness to others and its participation in the common creating of meaning.

Sartre stresses the sheer spontaneity of consciousness as a continual wrenching of consciousness away from itself, and considers this self-diremption as the source of temporality. Merleau-Ponty, on the other hand, emphasizes that spontaneity is itself a primary acquisition, and that temporalization is inseparably passivity and activity. Thus subjectivity is temporality, but the subject does not personally initiate temporalization any more than it chooses being born. As temporality, the subject finds itself always already situated in the world; yet the world does not come into being as a world in the absence of a subject projected towards it. Temporality is the basis of our spontaneity – rather than *vice versa* – because we are given to ourselves as a pre-personal project already in process, that is, as a temporality already temporalizing itself. Our existence as temporality precludes our being an absolute consciousness; rather, our own temporal perspectivity opens the way for other equally perspectival subjects and for the genesis of meaning in our intersubjective experience. As Merleau-Ponty notes, the common conception of time implicitly identifies meaning and temporality insofar as it considers everything which is meaningful for our present concerns to be 'part of our present'. Once we identify subjectivity with temporality, we moreover rule out a meaning created by an absolute reason. Thus we saw that the common conception of time as a river slips in the assumption of a situated perceiver without whom the stream could not even have a direction. Temporality is therefore inseparable from being-in-the-world; and meaning is inseparable from the primary directionality which that primordial inherence in the world implies. The French word *'sens'* captures especially well this interdependence of directionality and meaning. Having identified temporality as subjectivity, we can therefore go on to identify these with meaning and thus to declare that temporality is the meaning (*'sens'*) of our existence. Once again, we are brought to the realization that subject and world are inseparably connected through the primordial project and that the alternative of realism or idealism must be rejected in favour of a phenomenological description of our being-in-the-world.

In light of our phenomenological description of temporality as self-affecting subjectivity which is primordially self-aware, we are now able to recognize that subject and object are 'abstract "moments" ' of a unique concrete totality which is *'presence'*. The problems raised by objective thought therefore resolve themselves definitively. For example, the structure of *'presence'* replaces the Cartesian dilemma of a mechanistic body incomprehensibly causally connected to an immaterial soul. Once that 'the world *"in itself" '* is identified with the temporal horizons, and the *'for-itself'* with 'the hollow in which time is formed', the dichotomy of the formerly irreconcilable terms is replaced with the single indivisible project of temporalization. And just as the future is inherently that of a certain present, so the for-itself (or, consciousness) is inherently that of a certain actually existing body. Our actual experience of being *present* in the world discloses that our phenomenal body is essentially a *knowing* body; thus the traditional body-soul problem vanishes. Similarly, the identification of temporality with subjectivity undercuts the question regarding the nature of the world prior to the evolution of human consciousness. Given our earlier remarks about the interdependence of temporality, subjectivity and meaning, it is evident that this sort of question is, strictly speaking, meaningless. As we have seen, the world is inseparable from a human perspective and to pretend otherwise is invariably to reintroduce the human subject 'by the back door', so to speak. Finally, the identification of time and the subject opens us to other people. We saw earlier that we are linked to others via behaviour, that is, by witnessing their 'presence in the world'. In virtue of our fuller understanding of the meaning of 'presence' (as being simultaneously presence to ourselves and involvement in the world), we are now in a position to appreciate how others are present to us, and we to them. We have seen that our own self-awareness is inevitably fraught with ambiguity, that we are present to ourselves without ever coinciding completely with ourselves. It consequently becomes comprehensible that others can be present to us, that the projects which we *are* can interweave in an intersubjective field of presence. The pre-objective world in which we are always already involved is thus a social world; and since we have renounced the solipsistic supremacy of the transcendental ego, we will need to reconsider the actual extent of our freedom.

Notes

1. See Sartre, *Being and Nothingness: a Phenomenological Essay on Ontology*, 'Introduction': 'The Pursuit of Being': 'Being-In-Itself, pp. 24–30; 'Part One': 'The Problem of Nothingness': 'The Phenomenological Concept of Nothingness'. and 'The Origin of Nothingness', pp. 49–85; 'Part Two': 'Being-For-Itself ': 'Temporality', pp. 159–237.
2. *Being and Nothingness*: 'Introduction': 'The Pursuit of Being', pp. 3ff.

3

Freedom

We have seen that our experience of *'presence'* precludes our being causally connected to our body, world or society; hence we have already undercut determinism and taken our stand on the side of freedom. But how are we to describe this freedom? At first glance it would seem that we have unwittingly committed ourselves to the Sartrian view of freedom articulated in *Being and Nothingness*. Sartre's account rejects the transcendental ego in favour of a non-coinciding, situated, temporalizing subjectivity which has a body and finds itself engaged with others 'in an already meaningful world'. This being-in-the-world involves contingency, ambiguity and objective limits.[1] Nevertheless, Sartre's position is fundamentally at odds with that of Merleau-Ponty, since the Sartrian subject is an *absolute* freedom *confronting* others in a situation of inevitable and inescapable *alienation*.[2] Not surprisingly, therefore, Merleau-Ponty's chapter on freedom comprises an extensive critique of Sartre's position.

Merleau-Ponty opens his analysis with an investigation of the phenomenon of *'presence'* which emerged as pivotal in the last chapter and which Sartre himself considers requisite for freedom.[3] In *Being and Nothingness* Sartre argues that consciousness cannot be self-identical plentitude because that would relegate it to the order of the in-itself, or non-conscious being. If it is to exist at all, consciousness must be self-consciousness even at the pre-reflective level; in short, consciousness must exist 'as a presence to itself '. Besides being-for-itself, consciousness exists as being-for-others, as its experience of shame indicates; moreover, these two modes of existence are equally fundamental for Sartre. In its very upsurge as for-itself, consciousness finds itself in the presence of others. Being-for-itself and being-for-others are incommensurable however, and consciousness remains incapable of relating what it is in the intimacy of its own presence to itself with what it is for others.[4] For itself, consciousness escapes all objectification because its being as consciousness is antithetical to the being of objects. In reflection, consciousness therefore discovers a pre-personal unqualified flux, a limitless generality, a pure spontaneity unfettered by any characteristics whatsoever. For itself, consciousness is absolute; it is pure presence – neither a male, nor a clerk, nor a Jew, nor French, nor crippled, nor ugly, nor sophisticated. These various characteristics are conferred by other people who – precisely because they are other – inevitably impose an external perspective, thereby reducing consciousness to the status of an object endowed with determinate qualities. Of course, the being-in-itself which it is for others presupposes that consciousness exists 'as body in the midst of the world'; moreover, Sartre acknowledges that the for-itself can regard itself as having specific traits by adopting the objectifying view of an other. Nevertheless, its very awareness prevents it from ever simply *being* that being. Since it finds itself in a world inhabited by other people, the for-itself cannot get rid of its being-for-others – but it alone chooses its attitude towards the latter. Sartre contends that the for-itself can always destroy the other's alienating look by objectifying the other with *its* look. It thereby gains the advantage over the other, albeit never definitively because the other can reassert its freedom at any time. Yet the mere fact that it apprehends the other as threatening indicates that the for-itself freely posits the other's freedom. Even the masochistic attempt to restrict itself to being solely an object for the other is a choice in which the for-itself reaffirms its own existence as freedom.[5]

Sartre's account is by no means easy to refute, as *Being and Nothingness* in its entirety constitutes an intricate argument for the absolute freedom of human reality; moreover, Sartre himself anticipates and counters a number of objections. To those who would challenge the alleged absoluteness of freedom, he responds that only things can be acted upon. Sartre argues that questioning presupposes the questioner's absolute freedom; consequently, critics already subvert their arguments against such a freedom in questioning his position. Sartre's point is that 'a nihilating withdrawal' from the given is the necessary condition for all questions whatsoever – an utter identity of the questioner with the questioned would preclude any question ever arising. In questioning, the questioner detaches himself from the being which he is questioning and thus is not subject to its causality. The questioner 'wrenches' himself from the questioned 'in order to be able to bring out of himself the possibility of a non-being' – for example, the possibility that Sartre's account is *not* correct. This non-being is indescribable because nothingness is not a thing, but it supposes being because it is always the nothingness of something. As being-in-itself is 'full positivity', it cannot be the origin of nothingness; instead, the latter must come to the world through a being which is its own nothingness – otherwise we fall into an infinite regress. A consideration of the meaning of questioning reveals that the questioner brings nothingness to the world. Sartre concludes that the human being – the being which questions – must be freedom. Sartre's reasoning is that the human being must 'secrete' its own nothingness if it is to be the being through which nothingness comes to the world. Secretion of nothingness requires rupture with the causality of being-in-itself and this rupture is freedom. Further, the human being cannot first exist and then become free; on the contrary, freedom must be the very being of human reality.[6] To postulate a potential or partial freedom is to rule it out altogether by making human reality being-in-itself – in short, a thing rather than a being which is present to itself.

At this stage the reader may be strongly tempted to dismiss Sartre's account and Merleau-Ponty's subsequent critique, on the grounds that the former has simply missed the point of the traditional debates concerning free will versus determinism. It is therefore important to note that Sartre himself anticipates such an objection and reverses it in response. As he sees it, the customary discussions are tiresome and superficial because they stop short of the fundamental question. By way of illustration Sartre observes that the advocates of free will look for decisions which lack a preceding cause, or for deliberations about two antithetical but equally possible acts whose causes and motives are of exactly equal weight. For their part, the determinists retort that all actions are caused and that even the most trifling gestures refer to causes and motives from which they derive their significance. In denying this, the free will advocates destroy the necessary intentional structure of the act and render action absurd. The determinists on the other hand fail to investigate the intentionality of action – they content themselves with designating causes and motives without bothering to inquire how these 'can be constituted as such'.[7]

Sartre therefore undertakes a close phenomenological analysis of causality and motivation. In light of the explication provided earlier, it is clear that he rejects any notion that there are external or internal factors which simply impinge on human reality.

According to Sartre, something which is not *experienced* as a cause cannot *be* a cause. Yet although he repudiates the traditional conceptions of causality and motivation, Sartre retains the terms 'cause' and 'motive' and incorporates them into his position. Thus he agrees with the determinists' contention that any act must have a motive, but he rejects their conclusion that the latter causes the act. Instead, Sartre argues that by its very upsurge as freedom the for-itself organizes undifferentiated being-in-itself into a world, and any particular act is an expression of this fundamental project. By its choice of end, the act 'carves out' the world's particular objective structure and effects the emergence of a cause; for the latter is simply 'the objective apprehension' of that situation as it is disclosed in light of the particular end as 'able to serve as the means for attaining this end'. The cause in no way determines the action, since it is 'only in and through the project of an action' that it appears at all, and the same can be said for the motive. As consciousness must be present to itself, the consciousness of a cause must be non-thetic self-consciousness. Sartre declares that 'the motive is nothing other than the apprehension of the cause in so far as this apprehension is self-consciousness', and he concludes that cause, motive and end are inseverable terms of a project which is itself a particular way of being-in-the-world – in short, a freedom.[8]

Commonly we consider causes and motives as external and internal givens, respectively. Thus, for example, we speak of being forced to do one thing and prevented from doing another, or being inclined to take a certain decision and prompted to abandon another. Sartre clearly rejects these reifications. Being forced or prevented is tantamount to being acted upon, and such passive existence of a for-itself is unthinkable. Similarly, inclinations and promptings cannot act on us in any way, for that would convert us into things. Action is the being of human reality; moreover, action must be strictly autonomous if it is to be action rather than mere movement. The for-itself is 'a nihilating spontaneity'; as such, its determination to action must itself be action and the latter must be a ceaseless 'surpassing of the given' toward a chosen end. Consequently, motives, feelings, passions, temperament or character cannot exist as givens in human reality. Contrary to common conceptions, consciousness does not admit of any contents, nor freedom of any attenuation. Since freedom is the very being of human reality, it is as senseless to speak of degrees of freedom as it is to predicate degrees of existence. Sartre explains that feelings and passions are not things but ways of being-in-the-world, while temperament or character belongs to the for-itself's being-for-others – which in turn depends upon the for-itself's freely chosen mode of relating to those others. We usually regard choice as a decision following a voluntary deliberation in which we assess the relative weight of various motives; but Sartre argues that such a conception is quite misleading. In fact, deliberation is itself a chosen conduct, and the resulting reflective decision is a second-ary choice within the fundamental choosing which is our very existence as freedom. This primordial project causes the emer-gence of motives and determines their weight, while deliberation merely serves to bring them to our attention. Thus the commonly alleged weakness of our will in no way undermines our 'original, ontological freedom' – on the contrary, the former is simply a manifestation of the choice which we make of ourselves.[9]

Are there then no obstacles or limits, and are we to conclude that freedom is pure caprice? Sartre explicitly warns against such a misinterpretation by pointing out that freedom could not exist without obstacles or limits, and that a capricious freedom would be no freedom at all. As a nihilating spontaneity, the for-itself clearly requires that there be something to be nihilated; or to put it somewhat differently, a perpetual surpassing of the given sup-poses that there be a given to be surpassed. By its very structure as project, choice precludes instantaneity and rules out the possibil-ity of our existing without a past. Sartre readily concurs with common sense in maintaining that our past commitments weigh on us – even to the point of 'devouring' us – and that a prisoner is evidently not always free to leave the prison, nor a paraplegic to get up and walk. In Sartre's estimation however, common sense errs when it goes on to equate freedom with the ability to obtain one's chosen ends. Physical, social, political and religious free-doms are in fact supported by ontological freedom, and Sartre's analysis concerns itself exclusively with the latter.

Ontological freedom, that is, 'autonomy of choice', is in-distinguishably choosing and acting; but Sartre insists that choos-ing does not mean wishing or obtaining. In failing to uphold the difference, the common sense conception of freedom inadver-tently collapses the distinction between our waking life and the nocturnal world of our dreams. Instantaneous transformations of ourselves and the world typically occur in our dreams, giving them their air of unreality – thus our merest wish suffices to produce the desired object or to annihilate any apparent obstacle. On waking however, we find ourselves once more in the real world with all its substantial restrictions. Sartre contends that these restrictions are essential, because an unrestricted choice would be no choice at all; moreover, it would be absurd to maintain that freedom simply creates its own obstacles. Our freedom is in fact paradoxical: 'there is freedom only in a *situation*, and there is a situation only through freedom'. Everywhere we encounter resistances and obstacles which we have not created, but it is we ourselves who confer meaning on them by our very existence as freedom. Sartre's famous example of the crag illustrates the point: the rock face reveals itself as unclimbable only within a project of climbing. For the injured or would-be mountaineer it presents an obstacle; for the seasoned climber it provides an opportunity to set a new record, while for the airborne tourist it offers the chance to take a striking photograph. Of course, not every crag will lend itself to being climbed – that depends on 'the brute being' of the crag – but it can disclose its resistance only within the context of a human project. Thus 'there is no obstacle in an absolute sense'; nor can we ever separate out what comes from 'the brute given' and what from freedom in any particular case. Without the brute *'quid '*, freedom could not exist; but by its very upsurge, freedom endows the brute being with meaning and value according to the choice which it makes of itself. Any limits which freedom encounters with reference to its past, its body, its place, its environment and other people, are therefore ultimately self-imposed. Although it is not free to *not* be free, 'freedom is total and infinite.'[10]

As Merleau-Ponty sees it, such a conception utterly destroys freedom. If freedom is our very being, so that it is the same no matter what we do or how we feel, then it becomes impossible to discern its appearance anywhere. A freedom which is infinite and omnipresent lacks any background of non-freedom from which to stand out; hence it cannot *be* anywhere. If all acts are free, then effectively none is free and the very idea of choice and action disappears. There is nothing to acquire if freedom is primordial and every instant finds us equally free; consequently, there is nothing to choose and nothing for us to do. Freedom cannot come into play anywhere or find expression in anything. If freedom is action as Sartre claims, then it is necessary that our decisions accomplish something and set a direction for the future, rather than leaving us 'just as indeterminate' the next instant. This does not mean of course that we renounce our power to interrupt and set a new direction – but that power implies our power to commence. Sartre himself rejects the notion that consciousness is reducible to a series of instants; moreover, he stresses that there must be a past, resistances and 'a commencement of realization in order that the choice may be distinguished from the dream and the wish'.[11] Yet are these stipulations not ultimately incompatible with the notion of a primordial, total and infinite freedom? How can such a freedom have an abode and a *field* in which to realize its objectives? In short, how can we ever experience freedom?

While agreeing with Sartre's criticism of the classical conception of free will, Merleau-Ponty detects an unresolved difficulty in the Sartrian notion of a global choice of ourselves and our whole way of being-in-the-world. If, as Sartre insists, that choice is synonymous with our very upsurge in the world, then it is unclear how it can be considered to be our choice at all. The very idea of such an initiatory choice is contradictory, inasmuch as choice implies an antecedent commitment. If, on the other hand, the Sartrian global choice is genuinely a choice of ourselves, then it must be a total modification of our existence which, once again, presupposes a prior acquisition to be converted by that choice. Sartre's definition of freedom as perpetual rupture or secreting of nothingness is therefore merely the negative feature of our global commitment to, and involvement in, a world. Sartre contends that freedom cannot be 'a simple undetermined power' but rather, that it must determine 'itself by its very upsurge as a "doing"'.[12] Nevertheless, Merleau-Ponty concludes that this 'ready-made freedom' reduces itself 'to a power of initiative' which must take up one of the world's propositions in order to become a doing. Merleau-Ponty maintains that 'concrete and actual freedom' lies in this transformatory exchange.

The very notion of an *exchange* precludes Sartre's conception of an entirely centrifugal signification. Sartre declares that human reality confers meaning on the brute given, and that 'nothing comes to it either from the outside or from within which it can *receive or accept*'. Further, he asserts that 'since freedom is a being-without-support and without-a-springboard, the project in order to be must be constantly renewed. I choose myself perpetually . . .'.[13] Charging that Sartre's position is ultimately indistinguishable from classical idealism, Merleau-Ponty rejects the notions of exclusively centrifugal signification and perpetual choice. Since Sartre's own distinction between dreaming and waking life attests to the fact that freedom requires a field, signification must be both centripetal and centrifugal. Merleau-Ponty therefore reconsiders Sartre's example of the crag to show how this can be so. He acknowledges that only the presence of a human being and a project of scaling can confer attributes such as 'unclimbable' on the rock. However, Sartre himself admits that given a project of scaling, some rocks will prove more favourable than others. Consequently, it is in virtue of my freedom that there are obstacles and means in general, but my freedom does not determine the world's particular contours. Merleau-Ponty draws attention to the fact that irrespective of any specific intention to scale them, these crags will strike me as being high simply 'because they exceed my body's power to take them in its stride'. Although I may imagine myself a giant, the 'natural self' prevents my actually making the mountains minute for me. Besides, even 'my express intentions' are evidently modelled on the pre-reflective experience of those 'general intentions' which my natural self sustains around me and which affect my environment independently of any decision on my part. These bodily intentions are general in that they hold for all similarly organized 'psycho-physical subjects' and 'constitute a system' which simultaneously includes 'all possible objects' – for example, if the crag looks high and straight, the pine looks small and bent. Thus Gestalt psychology has been able to demonstrate that there are particular shapes which other people and I especially favour. In addition, there are various ambiguous shapes suggesting perpetually shifting significances, which elicit our 'spontaneous evaluations'. A pure consciousness or an absolute freedom could not sustain such ambiguity, but would immediately coincide with the objects of its intentions without ever experiencing their distance in a shared world. Obstacles come to be such not by any acosmic conferring of meaning, but by a pre-reflective exchange between 'our incarnate existence' and the world.

This exchange, which constitutes the basis for all deliberate acts of signification, is not restricted to 'external perception' but informs any evaluation whatsoever. Sartre is therefore correct in arguing that far from acting on my freedom as causes, suffering and fatigue have a meaning and express my manner of being-in-the-world. Moreover, if that original choice involves a refusal to tolerate suffering and fatigue, then a decision to continue hiking despite my pain and weariness will exact a considerable price – for it will require a different way of existing my body and thus, 'a radical conversion of my being-in-the-world'. Nonetheless, Sartre's repeated insistence on the importance of the past does not suffice to show how a frequently confirmed attitude comes to acquire 'a favoured status', so that the adoption of an opposite attitude becomes increasingly improbable.[14] Since the Sartrian freedom is absolute, any habitual modes of being-in-the-world must be equally fragile at every moment. Consequently, habits cannot become sedimented in our life and any complexes which we have developed over time can always be readily dispelled in an instant by our freedom. Probability therefore becomes meaning-less – at best, it is reduced to a matter of statistics. However, this betrays our actual experience of having committed ourselves to something which subsequently weighs on us and lends a certain atmosphere to our present. Besides, we have already encountered probability and generality as phenomena of the perceived world which emerge through an interaction of the natural self and the world. In that exchange, a human level and a field of possible actions come into being. We must therefore reject Sartre's claim 'that two solutions and only two are possible: either man is wholly determined . . . or else man is wholly free'. We must refuse the Sartrian alternative of 'a nihilating spontaneity' on the one hand, and 'mechanical processes' on the other, 'each one in its incommu-nicable solitude'.[15] Instead, we must describe how our freedom gears itself to our situation and how that open situation summons, but does not dictate, especially favoured forms of response.

A consideration of how we relate to history will disclose the same need to go beyond the Sartrian alternative of absolute freedom or mechanistic causality to a third type of existence, which is that of an incarnate subjectivity. In his effort to refute determinism, Sartre argues that reflection reveals that in my pure presence to myself, I am an impersonal, 'pre-human flux' without any qualities whatsoever. Although I can subsequently consider myself a worker, for example, I can never fully *be* a worker. My awareness of being a worker remains second order; for myself, as opposed to my being-for-others, I am a pure consciousness freely evaluating itself as proletarian. A study of history shows that my objective place in production never suffices to kindle class-

consciousness and that revolt is therefore not the result of objective conditions. On the contrary, the worker evaluates the present
through his 'free project for the future', and becomes a proletarian
by deciding 'to will revolution'. His decision requires 'a pure
wrenching away from himself and the world', which enables him
to 'posit his suffering as unbearable suffering and consequently
[to] *make of it the motive* for his revolutionary action'. The worker
'wrenches' himself away from his past in order to evaluate it in the
light of the future and 'confer on it the meaning which *it has* in
terms of the project of a meaning which it *does not have*'.[16]
However, Sartre's position seems to deprive history itself of any
meaning save that which our will confers. Thus his criticism of
objective thought takes the form of an idealist reflection which
likewise overlooks the phenomena. Whereas objective thought
makes class-consciousness the product of objective conditions,
Sartre's analytic reflection makes the objective conditions dependent on a constituting consciousness, so that 'being a workman'
becomes reduced to the awareness of being one. Both objective
thought and idealist reflection deal with abstractions which miss
our actual existence; consequently, Merleau-Ponty invites us to
embark on a truly existential approach to the phenomenon of
class-consciousness.

At the outset, Merleau-Ponty cautions us not to seek either the
causes of class-consciousness or the conditions which make it
possible. As Sartre emphasizes, no external cause can act on a
consciousness; furthermore – as Sartre unfortunately fails to see –
it is a matter of discerning the conditions which actually elicit
class-conciousness, rather than those of its mere possibility. Using
'a genuinely existential method', we discover that my awareness
of being a worker or a bourgeois is not simply a function of the fact
that I market my labour or that I have a vested interest in
capitalism. Nor do I become proletarian or middle class the day I
decide to regard history from the perspective of the class struggle.
Instead, it is first of all a matter of *existing* as proletarian or middle
class; and this way of interacting with society and the world
motivates my revolutionary or counter-revolutionary projects, as
well as my express judgement that I am a proletarian or a
bourgeois. Motivation does not mean causation however; therefore, it is impossible to deduce my projects and judgements from
my life-style or vice versa. Neither impersonal forces nor an
unmotivated intellectual exercise renders me a worker or a bour-

geois. What makes me the one or the other is my manner of being-in-the-world within a socio-economic order which I experience and live.

Merleau-Ponty provides a detailed example of the genesis of class-consciousness by considering the lives of a factory worker, a tenant farmer and a day-labourer. Without any choice or explicit evaluation, those doing the same sort of job under comparable conditions 'co-exist in the same situation' and feel a certain kinship. This can simply continue without developing into class-consciousness and revolutionary activity or alternatively, various events can help to bring about such a transformation. The news of a factory workers' strike elsewhere and the resulting wage hike here, may sharpen the factory worker's perception of the established order. Seeing prices rise and feeling his own livelihood thus become precarious, the day-labourer may blame the town workers, so that class-consciousness fails to emerge. If such consciousness arises, it is not because the day-labourer decides to turn into a revolutionary and thereby bestows 'a value upon his actual condition', but because he has perceived concretely that his own life gears into that of the town workers and that they all participate in a common condition. For his part, the tenant farmer may begin to identify with the factory workers on learning that the owner of his farm sits on the board of various industrial enterprises. In these ways, a sphere of the exploited begins to emerge in the social space and a regrouping beyond ideological and occupational identities becomes increasingly evident. This, then, is the coming-into-being of class-consciousness, and when the different segments of the proletariat experience their objective connection as a common impediment to each one's existence, a revolutionary situation obtains.

Merleau-Ponty, implicitly taking Sartre to task, insists that at no point is there a need for 'a *representation* of revolution', for each proletarian to think of himself expressly as such, for any deliberate evaluation or any 'explicit positing of an end'. It suffices that there be a feeling of solidarity among the various peasants and workers, and a sense of being involved in trying to change things. Both the established order and its destruction 'are lived through in ambiguity' – which is not to say that the proletarians and peasants unconsciously produce revolution, or that the latter is the result of 'blind, "elementary forces" ' manipulated by a handful of sly agitators. In reality, the alleged rabble-rousers' slogans are eagerly taken up in a revolutionary situation 'because they crystallize what is latent' in the workers' lives at large. In many respects, the making of a revolution is akin to the creating of an artistic work: both are neither blind nor transparent activities but rather, ambiguous undertakings whose meaning develops as the activity unfolds and whose outcome is neither foreseeable nor ever explicitly posited in advance. Both the artistic work and the revolutionary movement are intentions which create their own instruments and modes of expression. The revolutionary project matures at the pre-reflective level of my interactions with other people and my relations to my job, long before it becomes articulated and linked to objective goals. Thus when I take a stand *vis-à-vis* a possible revolution, thereby recognizing myself as a proletarian or a bourgeois, the adopting of that position is neither an automatic effect of my class status nor an instantaneous evaluation *ex nihilo*.

In Merleau-Ponty's judgement, Sartre's error lies in his exclusive focus on intellectual projects to the neglect of the existential project. As a consequence, Sartre's analysis overlooks all the rich ambiguity in the emergence of class-consciousness from the enigmatically lived-through experience of its prospective members. The unrepresented, ambiguously apprehended objective towards which their lives are polarized, stands in stark contrast to the thought object of the Sartrian constituting consciousness. In making class-consciousness the product of a decision and choice, Sartre disregards genuine intentionality and effectively declares that problems are instantly resolved. As Merleau-Ponty notes however, the intellectual project is itself the outcome of an existential project and expresses a particular manner of being-in-the-world. Like the proletarian or the peasant, the intellectual is in fact firmly rooted in co-existence, and the meaning, direction and future which he gives to his life spring from the way in which he lives that co-existence. Any conceptualization on his part comes from the same source; hence all attempts to derive actual existence from acts of consciousness are profoundly misguided. Being a bourgeois or a proletarian is not merely being aware of being the former or the latter. It means identifying oneself as the one or the other through a tacit or existential project which blends with one's manner of structuring the world and co-existing with others.

Sartre would of course counter this critique of his position by pointing out that while my being-for-others includes attributes such as proletarian or bourgeois, I am simply a pure consciousness for myself and can regard myself as proletarian or bourgeois only by adopting an outsider's perspective. Furthermore, it is impossible to deduce the other's presence from the ontological structure of being-for-myself (the for-itself), for that would destroy the other's otherness as a subjectivity irreducible to mine. The other's presence is therefore an original fact, and my experience of being in sympathy or community with others (the *Mitsein*) presupposes my experience of being in confrontation with them. In short, being-with-others is based on being-for-others, and 'conflict is the original meaning of being-for-others'. The experience of 'we' is 'extremely unstable', continually giving way again to the alienating experience of being-for-others. Fundamentally, my relation with others is one in which I attempt to 'enslave' them while they simultaneously seek to 'enslave' me.[17] Merleau-Ponty anticipates such a rejoinder and endeavours to forestall it. He argues that Sartre's radical dichotomy between being-for-myself and being-for-others precludes my ever experiencing the other. I can never recognize another subjectivity unless my being-for-myself already incorporates the structures of my being-for-others. In any case, the Sartrian being-for-others cannot account for all the features of my actual experience which an existentialist analysis brings to light. Other people are neither necessarily, nor ever entirely, objects for me; moreover, absolute subjectivity is purely an abstraction, and 'the-other-as-object' is an inauthentic characterization of others. A genuinely radical reflection shows that from the start, I must be aware of being somehow centred 'outside myself', of having an aura of generality about 'my absolute individuality'. Without there being such a primordial 'atmosphere of "sociality"' around my presence to myself, attributes such as male or bourgeois could have no meaning for me. Unless there were a primordial background of being-for-others, being-for-myself could not *emerge* as such and hence, I could not *be*. There must be a meaning beyond that which I constitute; there must be an intersubjectivity; and I must be anonymous in the double sense of being wholly individual and completely general.

If we adopt Sartre's account as opposed to Merleau-Ponty's, we effectively rule out any meaning, direction or truth of history – we rule out situations altogether. If becoming a worker or a bourgeois were a matter of pure initiative, history would lack any shape or structure, revolutionary situations or times of retrenchment would not exist, uprisings could reasonably be expected at any moment and statesmen would be indistinguishable from adventurers. In his eagerness to disprove the mechanistic view of history, Sartre overlooks the fact that history must have a meaning which is not simply conferred on it by human fiat – that it must be *'lived through'*. The meaning of events is neither a mental construct nor the inadvertent consequence of their simultaneity; rather, it is the actual intersubjective 'project of a future' which is prepared within anonymous co-existence prior to any personal decision. Signification is thus at once centrifugal and centripetal: we bestow history's meaning, but it itself puts that meaning forward. The individual is not the director of history; yet at a certain moment of its genesis, an individual can take up and carry forward the meaning which has been maturing in social co-existence. Since history offers a meaning to be taken up, we can discern historical truth and distinguish between the adventurer and the statesman.

The individual is born into a world in which significances already fashioned qualify him as male and bourgeois, for example, even in his presence to himself. Moreover, what has traditionally been considered a strictly individual experience – for instance, the seeing of a colour or the thinking of an idea – is only apparently unique; in actual fact, it draws on the social world. My concrete interactions with others familiarize me with 'a world of colours', so that a certain one stands out from a background for me. Consequently, even in colour perception I do not apprehend myself as a pre-human flux. My allegedly private thought similarly feeds on intersubjective life in that it supposes a particular cultural world. I am therefore not an inaccessible subjectivity but rather, 'a field of presence' – to myself, other people and the world. Sartre's notion of freedom as the secreting of nothingness is ultimately hypocritical, for such a global refusal depends continuously on an acceptance: it is itself a certain way of being-in-the-world which is firmly rooted in a particular cultural tradition and participates in social co-existence. Sartre's claim about the origin of nothingness can thus be supplemented: 'it is through the world that nothingness comes into being'. Far from being perpetually without support, my freedom is always buttressed by others; and my global commitment in co-existence sustains my power to effect a perpetual rupture. Nor is that power tantamount to perpetual choice – for such choice would preclude the ambiguity and generality which an existentialist approach discloses.

Sartre's fundamental error consists in opposing the for-itself to the in-itself, with no mediator between them. He thus disregards our primordial bond with the world – our being not only *in* the world but also *of* it. It is not a matter of having to choose between determinism on the one hand and absolute freedom on the other, because we are neither things nor pure consciousnesses but instead, incarnate subjectivities inhering in a situation which we assume and modify. By way of a further example, Merleau-Ponty counters Sartre's discussion of the torturer and his victim. Sartre emphasizes that the tortured man's response 'is a spontaneous production'; that, utterly alone before his tormentor, the victim is absolutely free to choose the moment when he will 'beg for mercy'.[18] Merleau-Ponty, by contrast, stresses that the victim's refusal to submit to the torturer's demands is buttressed by his continuing experience of being-with-others and of being involved in a joint struggle. It is not a case of a pure consciousness coming to a solitary decision, but rather, a matter of a prisoner with his loves, memories and felt commitments, living-through a situation.

In conclusion, Merleau-Ponty notes that freedom requires some power, that that power is sustained by our commitments, and that no commitment can originate or issue in absolute freedom. We are thus always committed, but never absolutely so; and we live our commitments ambiguously before we ever thematize them. Our existential analysis of the phenomenon of presence has revealed, moreover, that we are in fact the very synthesis which Sartre ruled out as an impossibility – namely, that of being-in-and-for-ourselves. Along with our existence, we all receive a particular style which figures in everything we think and do. Our past, our temperament and our environment are aspects of the total psychological-historical structure which we are, and it is thanks to this structure that we can be free at all. As an 'intersubjective field' we are, as Saint-Exupéry noted, 'but a network of relationships'; and it is by assuming those relationships and carrying them forward, that we realize our freedom.

Notes
1. Sartre, *Being and Nothingness: a Phenomenological Essay on Ontology*, pp. 121, 598ff., 616ff., 641ff., 655, 678, 705.
2. Ibid., pp. 473, 474, 671ff., 700.
3. Ibid., pp. 124–7, 241ff., 250, 568.
4. Ibid., pp. 120–6, 298, 301–3, 474.
5. Ibid., pp. 471ff.
6. Ibid., pp. 33–6, 56–61, 70, 71, 84, 116, 120–6, 615–16. Note that Sartre uses the following terms more or less interchangeably here (although he does specify that consciousness is 'the instantaneous nucleus' of the human being): consciousness, being-for-itself, the for-itself, the human being, human reality, man.
7. Ibid., pp. 559, 563–4.
8. Ibid., pp. 564ff., 575ff.
9. Ibid., pp. 16, 567ff., 581ff., 594ff., 612ff., 620ff., 705ff.
10. Ibid., pp. 619ff., 625ff., 635ff., 645ff., 675ff.
11. Ibid., pp. 599ff., 618ff., 622, 637ff.
12. Ibid., pp. 567ff., 616, 624. It is interesting to note that Sartre says (p. 568): 'Human-reality is free because ... it is perpetually wrenched away from itself and because it has been separated by a nothingness from what it is and from what it will be.'
13. Ibid., pp. 568–9, 617, 652.
14. Ibid., pp. 584ff., 597–8, 637–47.
15. Ibid., pp. 570–1.
16. Ibid., pp. 561ff., 640ff., 654ff., 666ff.
17. Ibid., pp. 301ff., 340ff., 471ff., 534ff., 654ff. (See particularly pp. 472–5, 536–7, 553, 656.)
18. Ibid., pp. 523ff.

Conclusion: A Critical Assessment of Merleau-Ponty's *Phenomenology of Perception*

Merleau-Ponty's central concern in the *Phenomenology of Perception* is to prompt us to recognize that objective thought fundamentally distorts the phenomena of our lived experience, thereby estranging us from our own selves, the world in which we live and other people with whom we interact. Such thinking is not confined to a single discipline or to a particular philosophical tradition. On the contrary, not only is it common to the sciences, social sciences and humanities, but it underlies both realism and idealism and feeds on common sense itself. In exposing the bias of objective thought, Merleau-Ponty seeks to re-establish our roots in corporeality and the perceptual world, while awakening us to an appreciation of the inherent ambiguity of our lived experience.

The body is commonly deemed to be the locus of experience; hence Merleau-Ponty investigates traditional conceptions of the body, draws our attention to their inadequacies and urges us to abandon these classical objectifications. In place of the traditional approaches, he proposes that we regard the body as a dynamic synthesis of intentionalities which, by responding to the world's solicitations, brings perceptual structures into being in a ceaseless dialectic whereby both body and objects are constituted as such. Since this ongoing dialectical movement effects the emergence of cultural as well as natural objects, Merleau-Ponty proceeds to consider our experience of other people. The latter, he contends, are not inaccessible minds incomprehensibly inhabiting impenetrable mechanisms whose functioning induces us to infer the existence of other subjectivities confronting our own. To this traditional philosophy, Merleau-Ponty opposes a phenomenological description of the direct, pre-reflective communication of body-subjects sharing a perceptual field. Concluding that private subjectivity is itself rooted in this primordial dialogue of incarnate intentionalities, Merleau-Ponty enjoins us to reject the entrenched notion of an original, self-enclosed, self-sustaining subjectivity. He further submits the traditional absolute *cogito* to a radical reflection, thereby revealing an underlying tacit *cogito* and re-integrating thinking into an existential project. According to Merleau-Ponty, the temporalization implied in such a project transcends the traditional passivity–activity dichotomy and again discloses the body-subject as a third kind of being. Consequently, the freedom of that incarnate subjectivity is neither non-existent nor absolute, but features the same dialectical structure that already emerged in the phenomenological analysis of our most rudimentary perception.

Merleau-Ponty radicalizes phenomenology and offers a profoundly positive phenomenological–existential philosophy in tracing intentionality back to its source in corporeal subjectivity and showing the latter to be part of a continuous dialectical exchange with the world and other incarnate subjectivities. By acknowledging a spontaneous accord between sensing and understanding, and a non-conceptual harmony among subjects in aesthetic experience, Kant's *Critique of Judgement* already pointed the way beyond the Cartesian bifurcation of human reality with its consequent restriction of intentionality. As Merleau-Ponty notes in his 'Preface', Husserl's subsequent distinction between 'operative intentionality' and 'intentionality of act' developed Kant's insight and, in broadening the notion of intentionality, enabled phenomenology to 'become a phenomenology of origins'.[1] Nevertheless, Husserl stopped short of establishing the origin of intentionality in the situated body-subject, with the result that his own philosophy remained insufficiently radical.

Other philosophers in the phenomenological or existentialist tradition similarly failed to undertake a truly radical reflection – that is, their thought did not reach the actual roots of experience and thus involved unacknowledged assumptions. Hegel, for example, declared in his *Phenomenology of Mind* that 'sense-certainy is unaware that its essence is the empty abstraction of pure being'; that '*for us* (tracing the process) or in itself, the universal *qua* principle, is the essence of perception; and as against this abstraction, both the moments distinguished – that which perceives and that which is perceived – are what is non-essential'; that spirit is the content of experience and that the goal of its process of embodiment 'is Absolute Knowledge or Spirit knowing itself as Spirit'.[2] Heidegger's philosophy likewise failed to put the primacy on human reality, as is evident from his assertion that 'the essence of man is essential for the truth of Being, and apart from this truth of Being man himself does not matter'.[3] Thus Heidegger stressed that 'the essence of man rests in Being-in-the-World'; but by 'World' he meant 'the clearing of Being, wherein man stands out from his thrown essence'.[4] For their part, Kierkegaard, Jaspers and Marcel sternly criticized traditional philosophy as remote from concrete human life and emphasized, by contrast, the need to focus on actual experience and to recognize the philosopher's participation in a situation. Their attempts to articulate a genuinely concrete philosophy fell far short of this goal, however, because all three called for a leap of faith to an absolute designated, respectively, as 'God', 'the Encompassing', and 'transcendence itself ' or the 'presence' which makes itself felt in 'mystery' and whose recognition is 'only possible through a sort of radiation which proceeds from revelation itself '.[5] While firmly rejecting any leap of faith and achieving concreteness, the philosophies of Nietzsche and Camus, in turn, lacked comprehensiveness; and though attaining the latter as well, that of Sartre was flawed by dualism. In avoiding all these pitfalls, Merleau-Ponty's *Phenomenology of Perception* stands as a remarkable achievement.

By drawing attention to the serious shortcomings of objective thought and discussing these in detail, Merleau-Ponty encourages us to abandon the traditional approaches and return to the phenomena of our concrete experience. The *Phenomenoloy* not only provides a method whereby such a return can be accomplished, but also undertakes that return itself in its phenomenological–existential analyses of the body, objectivity, subjectivity, thought, time, intersubjectivity, freedom and history. Merleau-Ponty's treatment of these perennial issues suggests that we are primordially *of* the natural world and therefore fundamentally *at home* in it; that we similarly enjoy a pre-reflective *bond* with others and the human world; that by our daily lives we *participate* in shaping our world and determining the course of our joint history; that our commitments are never completely unsupported since our freedom is always *interwoven* with that of other people; and that the carnality and fundamental ambiguity of our being-in-the-world are by no means impediments to reflection or to communication with others.

To appreciate the full import of the *Phenomenology*'s orientation, it is instructive to recall Sartre's thesis in *Being and Nothingness* by way of comparison. Sartre contends that the phenomenon of *presence* is a *fall*, a *degeneration* of the in-itself; that any synthesis of a 'nihilating sponteneity' and 'mechanical processes' is impossible; that the for-itself is thrown into exile in an utterly *indifferent* in-itself; that 'adversity and utilizable instrumentality' is the primary meaning of things; that the for-itself's situation is one of *inevitable separation* from things and abandonment in a world which it seeks to *appropriate* by various techniques in a vain attempt to give itself a foundation; that the inherent contradiction in its fundamental project of appropriation renders the for-itself an utterly 'useless passion' and *dooms* all its activities to *equivalence*, so that solitary drinking and leading a country amount 'to the same thing'; that the basic project of appropriation likewise characterizes the for-itself's relations with others and inevitably imprisons it a circle of seeking to *enslave* and to escape such *enslavement* itself; that the for-itself's selfness requires *negating* the other; that unity with others is theoretically and practically *unrealizable*; that the very essence of relations with others is *insecurity, danger, confrontation* and *conflict*; that others inevitably *impose* an *alien* meaning and *limit* the for-itself's freedom; that the mere existence of others lends an indefeasible 'dimension of alienation' to the for-itself's situation; that an *inescapable alienation* thus characterizes all situations; that 'the very meaning' of *freedom* is to surge up in the world as 'confronting others' and to cause the emergence of a situation whose 'essential characteristic . . . is to be alienated'; that, finally, the for-itself's *alienated* being (its being-for-others) is its *link* with others.[6]

Sartre's notion of ontological freedom forms the core of his position; consequently, by uncovering the inherent contradiction in this pivotal concept, Merleau-Ponty effectively demolishes the very foundation of Sartre's philosophy. Although Merleau-Ponty devotes the final chapter of his *Phenomenology* to an analysis of freedom, his critique of Sartrian freedom actually constitutes a recurrent theme through the entire work. Of course, he frequently does not use the term 'freedom', but we have seen that at each stage of the inquiry Merleau-Ponty draws attention to the insoluble dilemmas incurred by reducing reality to a product of pure construction or mechanistic causality. In focusing on the underlying prejudice common to both approaches and on the need to recognize a third kind of existence which both reject, Merleau-Ponty systematically undermines Sartre's idea of a for-itself whose very being is freedom. He thereby simultaneously institutes a new way of thinking which, being more radical, discerns the derivative nature of the Sartrian notion of alienation and goes beyond it to disclose our primordial bond with the natural and human world.

We have seen in the previous chapters that the dichotomy of in-itself and for-itself is fatally flawed and that the Sartrian nihilation is itself rooted in a more basic tacit affirmation. Far from being cut off and paralyzed by an indifferent being-in-itself, we are primordially related to, and animated by, a pre-objective world which solicits our sensibilities and enables us to actualize and develop them. Being-in-the-world is therefore not an exile; and although we can indeed regard things as discreet, adverse entities to be seized through the application of techniques, such an attitude toward our environment depends on the anonymous dialectical movement in which the body-subject is intervolved with pre-objective being anterior to any separation. As it is not primordially apart from the world but rather of it and in fecund interaction with it, incarnate subjectivity is not inherently doomed to seek the appropriation of a foundation – nor are its activities condemned to equivalence. Moreover, its incarnate intentionality already opens the body-subject to other incarnate subjectivities and inaugurates a pre-personal dialogue which is mutually enriching. A fundamental mutual comprehension thus subtends any subsequent misunderstandings, so that our basic relations with others are not ones of confrontation but of co-operation. Prior to any refusal of others, our bodily being establishes a pre-personal unity with them; and it is in virtue of such unity that selfhood can develop at all. While it is true that others can impose alien meanings on us, their ability to do so and ours to apprehend them as alien, suppose a positive, pre-reflective reciprocity which rules out the alleged inevitability of alienation.

The importance of this radical reversal of the Sartrian position cannot be over-estimated. Far from being part of the human condition, alienation, confrontation, misunderstandings, conflicts, terror and a Hobbesian state of war thereby become contingent transformations of a basic harmony which impugns any cavalier dismissal of calls for global co-operation as mere pipe-dreams. The pervasive sense of alienation in the western world today becomes, by implication, a phenomenon calling for critique and rectification based on a re-awakened appreciation of primary perceptual reciprocity. The *Phenomenology* provides just the sort of comprehensive grounding which such a critique requires if it is to be philosophically compelling. Merleau-Ponty's step-by-step disclosure of our primordial inherence in the world also lays the foundation for an explicitly ecological approach to our environment and an accompanying development of an appropriate technology. Our fundamental belonging to, and dialectical interaction with, the natural world means that our neglect or destruction of the latter carries that of ourselves in its wake. Merleau-Ponty's critique of rationalism calls into question 'the placing of spirit in an axiological dimension having no common measure with nature' and prompts him 'to prepare the substructure of living experience without which reason and liberty are emptied of their content and wither away'.[7]

By restoring our rootedness in the perceived world and in pre-personal co-existence with others, the *Phenomenology* paves the way for a concrete morality which is adequate to the demands of our age. Any allegation that such a claim involves the naturalistic fallacy, falls prey itself to Merleau-Ponty's critique of the traditional fact-value distinction. The perceiver is neither an isolated, passive recipient of an in-itself *datum* nor a solitary, absolute artificer of a perceptual structure but instead, an incarnate subjectivity relating simultaneously centrifugally and centripetally to an intersubjective, emergent world. The ceaseless, dialectical co-structuring of a dynamic, perceptual field is already pre-reflectively value-laden and its phenomenological description brings to light value-facts which defy the classical dichotomy.[8] The recognition of this inextricable intertwining of facts and values in lived experience precludes our taking refuge in any abstract morality. As Merleau-Ponty indicates in his 1946 address defending the *Phenomenology* before the *Société français de philosophie*, his text effectively puts us *en route* to creating an ethics of genuine regard for others in the concreteness of our specific situation:

If we admit that our life is inherent to the perceived world and the human world, even while it re-creates it and contributes to

its making, then morality cannot consist in the private adherence to a system of values. . . . Thus we cannot remain indifferent to the aspect in which our acts appear to others. . . . It is the
very demand of rationality which imposes on us the need to act
in such a way that our action cannot be considered by others as
an act of aggression but, on the contrary, as generously meeting
the other in the very particularity of a given situation. . . . Just
as the perception of a thing opens me up to being . . . the
perception of the other founds morality . . .[9]

The social–political implications of that remark are only too
evident; and whilst the very structure of perception precludes
guarantees, Merleau-Ponty's description of perceptual experience
does indicate that successful co-existence is genuinely possible. In
overturning the Sartrian conception of freedom, the *Phenomenology* implicitly appeals to us to realize our responsibility in
actively seeking harmony with others in all aspects of our
existence.

In radicalizing the phenomenological reduction and implement-
ing it in a comprehensive investigation of perception, Merleau-
Ponty succeeds in uncovering the tacit assumptions in traditional
modes of thinking. In addition, he offers us a new way of
philosophizing whose implications are clearly very far-reaching.
The *Phenomenology of Perception* therefore constitutes an invalu-
able contribution not only to the philosophical discourse but also
to that of related disciplines. Despite its signal achievements
however, Merleau-Ponty's extraordinary text poses a number of
problems. Before proceeding to consider them, it is essential to
forestall potential misconceptions concerning the nature of such
an examination. There is a way of reading the *Phenomenology* from
the outside, so to speak, which merely serves to confirm us in our
prejudices. Such an approach typically deplores the general ambiguity of the work as well as its lack of precise definitions, succinct
explanations, telling refutations, straightforward arguments, convincing proofs or unequivocal demonstrations. At its extreme,
such an 'external' reading dismisses the entire text as unintelligible – an extended exercise in 'muddled thinking'. In its more
moderate form, this mode of critique attempts to sift out and
translate 'the interesting bits' into unambiguous philosophical
terminology before submitting them to closer scrutiny. In either
case, the critic operates with a whole host of preconceptions about

the meaning of 'good' philosophy and the criteria for its evaluation. The moderate critic furthermore takes for granted that in
philosophy, as opposed to poetry, content can be separated
from form – Nietzsche notwithstanding. Such a *modus operandi* is
profoundly uncritical, and it misses the very essence of the
Phenomenology altogether.

Merleau-Ponty's *Phenomenology of Perception* calls into question
our traditional conception of philosophy, our habitual categories
and criteria, even our established conceptual framework itself. In
the process of doing so, moreover, the *Phenomenology* is developing a fresh discourse, an innovative philosophy; consequently, we
must firmly resist the temptation to tailor it to the old constructs if
we are to appreciate what it is saying. In order to understand and
assess it, we must leave our various assumptions behind and open
ourselves to the text itself. We will also do well to keep in mind
Merleau-Ponty's own cautionary remarks about the status of the
work in his 'Introduction' to the *Phenomenology*. Throughout the
book, he implicitly stresses the inseparability of form and content
by continually drawing our attention to the weaknesses of both
the intellectualist and the empiricist reductions, and the consequent need for a third kind of being. In the chapter 'The Spatiality
of the Body Itself and Motility' Merleau-Ponty says explicitly that
matter and form stand in a relationship of '*Fundierung*', that 'form
integrates within itself the content until the latter finally appears
as a mere mode of form itself ' and that existence is a '.dialectic of
form and content'.[10] It is accordingly misguided, to say the least, to
assume that Merleau-Ponty's own philosophy can be detached
from its form; furthermore, we saw in the chapter 'The Body as
Expression and Speech' why the traditional theories of language
are ultimately untenable. Our predilection for divorcing the body
from the mind and the object from the subject, prompts us to
regard language as detachable from thought and meaning as
exclusively on the side of the latter. Merleau-Ponty's phenomenological analysis of language aims to awaken us to the phenomenon
of incarnate signification which rules out any such division and
imbues words with significance.

As in the case of the innovative speaker, the philosopher who
breaks new ground brings a novel meaning into being in the very
act of articulating it, and its expression – whether verbal or
written – is as inseparable from that meaning as are the works of
poets, musicians or painters from theirs. Through the style of

writing and choice of words, the creative philosopher gives birth to an existential significance which inhabits the words themselves instead of lying somewhere behind them. The words themselves, in short, are essential – they cannot simply be stripped away and others substituted to expose the philosopher's 'real' meaning. If that is the case, then our reading of the *Phenomenology* must not be a matter of unwrapping or decoding Merleau-Ponty's thought but rather, of rendering ourselves genuinely present to *its* presence in the text itself. As Merleau-Ponty notes, we 'begin to understand a philosophy by feeling [our] way into its existential manner, by reproducing the tone and accent of the philosopher'.[11] Even the summarizing of an authentic, or originating, philosophy is therefore fraught with difficulty and any assessment of that philosophy must be made strictly on its own terms.

An excellent starting point for evaluating the shortcomings of the *Phenomenology* lies in Merleau-Ponty's own estimation of the work shortly before his death. In one of his 'Working Notes' dated July, 1959 we find the following startling judgement: 'The problems posed in *Ph.P.* are insoluble because I start there from the "consciousness"–"object" distinction – –'.[12] By way of elaboration, Merleau-Ponty says (in the same note) that the entailment of a global disturbance by a certain physiological injury (as in the case of Schneider) remains incomprehensible given the aforementioned distinction, and that the purported '*objective* condition . . . is a way of expressing and noting an event of the order of brute or wild being which, ontologically, is primary. This event is that a given *visible* properly disposed (a body) hollows itself out an invisible sense ['*sens*'] – –'.[13] What are we to make of this cryptic note? Has not Merleau-Ponty at every step of his analysis in the *Phenomenology* endeavoured precisely to *overturn* the traditional distinction between 'consciousness' and 'object' by disclosing incarnate subjectivity as a *third kind of being* which is irreducible to either consciousness or objective body? Has he not reiterated that this third term is primordially *of* the world? Has he not taken pains to show – in his analysis of habitual behaviour, for example – that the body-subject *incorporates* the world's structures into its own space? Has he not insisted that the world is not to be regarded as a totality of *objects*, nor the subject as a spectator *consciousness* surveying the lot? Has he not emphasized repeatedly in the *Phenomenology* that there is a *genesis* of subject and object in pre-reflective perceptual experience? Has he not throughout his

study of perception drawn attention to the *distortions* stemming
from our adherence to the classical distinctions? Has he not
consistently attempted to illuminate the primordial experience
which antedates any such distinctions? As the answer to all these
questions cannot but be affirmative, it would seem that Merleau-
Ponty's own assessment of the *Phenomenology* must be discounted. Upon further reflection however, we shall see that this
conclusion is too hasty – for the issue itself is far more complex
than the foregoing would suggest.

In the *Phenomenology of Perception* Merleau-Ponty is concerned
to show that perception is not *imposition* – whether of an objective
datum on a passive subject or a subjective structure on an external
object – but rather, pre-reflective *communication* ('dialogue') *between* the perceived world and the perceiving body-subject.
Merleau-Ponty's choice of title is significant in this regard, for his
study encompasses perceiving and the percept – as the double
meaning of 'perception' indicates; moreover, his phenomenology
reveals that these two terms are inextricably and dynamically
interrelated in perceptual experience. We have seen, further, that
Merleau-Ponty's phenomenological description of perception
stresses the phenomenal body's primordial *anchorage* in and *bond*
with, the pre-objective world. This means that the perceiver is
simultaneously *part of* the perceived world and sufficiently *apart
from* it for dialogue *between* them to arise. The perceiver is
concurrently perceived and perceiving – but not in the sense of
the Sartrian 'look', as is evident from the preceding chapters. This
would suggest that in belonging to the perceived world, the
perceiver shares its fundamental *texture* while retaining the distinction of existing as a perceiving being – and a human one at
that. Further, Merleau-Ponty's tracing of meaning to a pre-
reflective *exchange* between incarnate subjectivity and pre-
objective being suggests that the *emergence* of meaning has to do
with this paradoxical difference-in-sameness, this transcendence
in immanence, which is the very essence of perception as
perceived-perceiving. Yet all this is – for the most part – latent in
the *Phenomenology*, as Merleau-Ponty concentrates on awakening
us to an awareness that all our so-called 'external' and 'internal'
perceptions – even our 'innermost' feelings and seemingly self-
subsistent thoughts – are the product of a ceaseless dialectical
interaction between the phenomenal body and the pre-objective
world. The focus here is on the existence of that fundamental

dialogue and on the way in which it structures the lived experience which subtends reflection itself. The aforesaid *paradox* which enables the dialogue to emerge at all and the actual *birth* of meaning thus remain largely unexplored.

In a very real sense, then, Merleau-Ponty's phenomenological description of perception starts from the everyday world of already acquired meanings and from the consciousness of an established, meaningful world. In its 'natural attitude' to the world – as we have seen – consciousness regards things as simply external entities, that is, as objects. Beginning with this everyday distinction of 'consciousness' and 'object', Merleau-Ponty seeks to alert consciousness to its primordial inherence in a body and strives to disclose the pre-reflective exchange whereby objects are constituted as such. Since this incarnate consciousness is an already perceiving, speaking, thinking subject situated and engaged in an already meaningful world, the *origin* of meaning remains perplexing – as does the exact nature of consciousness's inherence in body and world, given the dichotomous starting point which Merleau-Ponty himself acknowledges in the note cited earlier. As he admits there, the profound transformation which a given brain injury introduces into one's being-in-the-world accordingly remains puzzling in the *Phenomenology*.

Nonetheless, at various points in the work, Merleau-Ponty does begin to probe the birth of meaning and the paradoxical character of our being-in-the-world. In his study of the body's sexual being, for instance, he explores the coming into existence of sexual significance and the consequent need to reject the classical dichotomy of passivity and activity in describing the phenomenal body. Similarly, Merleau-Ponty's phenomenological investigation of expression and speech draws our attention to the difference between originating expression and everyday speech, and to the amorphous primordial silence from which a radically new meaning is born. The inception of a novel linguistic significance indicates the inadequacy of the traditional necessity-contingency and immanence–transcendence distinctions for understanding our actual manner of being-in-the-world. In the same chapter, Merleau-Ponty notes that there is an 'ever-recreated opening in the plenitude of being' which conditions all authentic expression; further, he likens this 'function which we intuit through language' to 'a wave', describes it as being 'its own foundation' and characterizes originating expression as a 'miracle'.[14] Elsewhere he describes how the phenomenal body adjusts to lighting in order to see, and how it transplants itself into things which it uses habitually (such as musical instruments, orthopaedic devices, items of clothing or transport vehicles) or how, by the same token, it incorporates the latter into its own bulk. These descriptions constitute implicit explorations of our paradoxical bond with the primitive, or universal, Being mentioned above.

The opening and closing sections of the *Phenomenology* are also significant in this respect, as they foreshadow the motifs of Merleau-Ponty's last writings. In his 'Preface' to the book, we learn that the phenomenologist strives to recapture the 'primitive contact with the world' so as to give it a philosophical standing; that phenomenological reflection discloses the world 'as paradoxical'; that 'the phenomenological world' is the meaning which shows through at the *intersection* of experience; that expression and language originate in 'the silence of primary consciousness'; that philosophy and art both endeavour to grasp the coming into being of meaning; that both are acts creating truth; that the world is 'the only pre-existent Logos' and that we ourselves are a 'network of relationships'.[15] The concluding 'Freedom' chapter reiterates that we are but such a network, and stresses that our primordial bond and exchange with the world reveal the need to discard the traditional passive–active dichotomy so that we may comprehend our being-in-the-world.

If we are to determine whether Merleau-Ponty's failure to develop these themes more fully significantly weakens his phenomenological description of perception, we must consider the nature of his final writings. At the time of his death, Merleau-Ponty was in the midst of working on a book which was intended to be an ontology of 'wild' or 'brute' Being and *Logos*. Among his 'Working Notes' of January 1959 there is one in which he makes it clear that he meant to reconsider, deepen and rectify the *Phenomenology* in this ontological investigation.[16] As it is, the project was brutally interrupted, leaving us only the following fragments: a half-finished manuscript predating 1952, whose third chapter appeared in modified form as the essay 'Le langage indirect et les voix du silence' ('Indirect Language and the Voices of Silence'), while the manuscript itself was published posthumously under the title *La prose du monde* (*The Prose of the World*);[17] the 1960 essay 'L'Œil et l'Esprit' ('Eye and Mind') which, according to M. Claude Lefort, provides 'a preliminary statement' of ideas to be developed

in the prospective ontology;[18] a manuscript comprising the introductory first part of Merleau-Ponty's projected book; and some
working notes. The latter manuscript and a selection of the notes
were published posthumously as *Le visible et l'invisible: suivi de
notes de travail* (*The Visible and the Invisible: Followed By Working
Notes*). Merleau-Ponty's 1960 '*Préface*' ('Introduction') to *Signes*
(*Signs*) also contains many of the themes which he planned to
elaborate in his ontology. Although it is of course impossible to
ascertain how the latter would actually have unfolded, we can
detect the general direction of Merleau-Ponty's later thought in
these pieces.

Earlier, I suggested that in the *Phenomenology* Merleau-Ponty
endeavours to draw our attention to the existence of a pre-
objective world underlying our scientific and common sense
views, a body-subject subtending our traditional conceptions of
the self, and a primary interaction persisting between this pre-
reflective self and pre-objective world. Accordingly, Merleau-
Ponty traces the traditional *cogito* to a bodily, tacit *cogito* operative
at the pre-reflective level of perceptual experience. In his later
work, he deliberately abandons this tacit *cogito*[19] and tries to reach
the level of silence below the distinction of 'consciousness' from
'intentional object' which even a tacit *cogito* implies. His aim is to
disclose the very emergence of meaning from 'brute' Being
through the wave-like 'coiling over' which makes our own flesh
'*self-sensing*'. Merleau-Ponty points out that this will require 'an
elucidation of philosophical expression itself . . . as the expression of what is before expression *and sustains it from behind*'. As
sensible we belong primordially to 'the flesh of the world', whilst
as sentient we hollow out a meaning without tearing any hole in
the tissue of brute Being; and 'all this is finally possible and means
something only because *there is* Being'. The latter, however, is not
in-itself but rather, comprises the whole perceptual world including ourselves. That world encompasses not only the visible, but
also its invisible substructure of brute Being – that dimension of
silence on which we draw in any act of authentic expression.[20]

Meaning is itself invisible; yet 'it appears only within' the
visible and is its 'secret counterpart'. In order to understand it, we
must comprehend the relation of silence to *Logos*, or originating
expression, in which truth 'speaks itself '.[21] To illuminate that
relation to Being which '[forms] itself *within Being*', Merleau-Ponty
returns again and again to the study of language and of art. He

attempts to show that far from being congealed inside or on top of the words, meaning inhabits them in such a way that the unity of spoken language is a unity of differences, a coherent system of 'determinate gaps' which is continually being reshaped by the network of speaking subjects. The latter bring new meanings into being from within the linguistic field by a movement of transcendence which modifies that field without ever leaving it behind.[22] Similarly, painters transform the visible from within it through a seeing which is at the chiasma of eye and mind. The painting of a self-portrait is an example *par excellence* of the 'coiling over' of vision which enables a new meaning to emerge from vertical Being. Simultaneously seer and seen, the painter belongs to the fabric of the visible and folds that fabric over so that a fresh meaning is hollowed out. The painter's vision is a seeing from within the visible itself – as such self-portrayal most readily shows. It thus becomes understandable that our own vision likewise 'installs' itself in things and that its power to do so points to a fundamental unity in the very tissue of Being. Merleau-Ponty puts it as follows in a note of September, 1959 in which he considers how best to describe pre-reflective Being.

> Take up again the analysis of the cube . . . to say that I have a view of it is to say that, in perceiving it . . . I go out of myself into it. I, my *view*, are caught up in the same carnal world with it; i.e.: my view and my body themselves emerge from the *same* being which is, among other things, a *cube* . . . It is hence finally the massive unity of Being as the encompassing of myself and of the cube, it is the wild, non-refined, 'vertical' Being that makes there be a cube. With this example grasp the upsurge of pure 'signification' – –[23]

The above passage shows just how far Merleau-Ponty has gone beyond his phenomenological description in the *Phenomenology of Perception*. What, if any, are the implications of this advance for an assessment of the *Phenomenology*? The answer hinges on what we take the task of phenomenology to be and that, in turn, depends to a considerable degree on whether – and how – we distinguish phenomenology from ontology, metaphysics and 'concrete' or existential philosophy as a whole. Unfortunately, Merleau-Ponty's own writings are rather unclear on these crucial points. Although a detailed discussion of the matter lies beyond the scope of this chapter, our evaluation of the *Phenomenology*'s shortcomings supposes an appreciation of the problem at issue. Briefly, the less definite the aforementioned distinctions are, the more significant is Merleau-Ponty's subsequent philosophizing in showing up inadequacies in his phenomenological description of perception.

The 'Preface' to the *Phenomenology* in fact opens with the question, 'What is phenomenology?' and the ensuing acknowledgement that an answer is in order. The entire 'Preface' constitutes Merleau-Ponty's reply. Thus we learn that phenomenology is indeed 'the study of essences' – such as 'the essence of perception' – but that it begins with our 'facticity' and reintegrates essences into existence. As a transcendental philosophy it brackets the claims springing from 'the natural attitude' to the world; yet it recognizes the pre-reflective presence of the world and devotes its whole efforts to re-establishing a 'primitive contact' with it and directly describing our actual experience. Merleau-Ponty admits that phenomology appears to say everything and to be incapable of defining its purview, but notes that it *'can be practised and identified as a manner or style of thinking'* which is attainable solely *via* 'a phenomenological method'. The latter, as we have seen, eschews scientific explanation and analytical reflection in favour of a description designed to re-awaken the primordial experience underlying all our reconstructions of the world. By putting in abeyance our common sense certainties and natural attitude, phenomenological reflection enables us to become aware of our presuppositions and restores a sense of 'wonder' *vis-à-vis* the world.[24]

The phenomenological reduction reveals 'the unmotivated upsurge of the world', its 'lived' unity and the impossibility of a thought which would encompass everything including itself. Since it discloses the irreducible facticity of both the world and our own reflection, 'the phenomenological reduction is that of an existential philosophy' and – as we saw earlier – phenomenology becomes 'a phenomenology of origins' which seeks to describe 'the core of existential [significance]', the unique style of existence expressed in the objects of its radical reflection.[25] Merleau-Ponty summarizes the nature of phenomenology and again explicitly equates it with existential philosophy in a 1947 essay on film and psychology:

Phenomenological or existential philosophy is largely an expression of surprise at this inherence of the self in the world and in others, a description of this paradox and permeation, and an attempt to make us *see* the bond between subject and world, between subject and others, rather than to *explain* it as the classical philosophies did by resorting to absolute spirit.[26]

Such a philosophy is synonymous with 'concrete thinking' and with a metaphysics which 'is the opposite of system'. Thus understood, metaphysics becomes the lucid awareness and description of our paradoxical being-in-the-world. Instead of constructing concepts to conceal the paradoxes of lived experience, metaphysics as Merleau-Ponty defines it rediscovers the 'fundamental strangeness' of the objects of our experience 'and the miracle of their appearing'.[27] As he points out in the 'Introduction' to *Signs*, this type of philosophy is the very antithesis of a 'God-like survey' and even of an allegedly 'higher point of view'. Instead of soaring over a world spread out beneath its gaze, 'it plunges into the perceptible', 'seeks contact with brute being' and – 'in regaining the "vertical" world' – discloses the 'chiasma of the visible'.[28]

Is not that, however, the task of his projected ontology as Merleau-Ponty outlines it in what has become *The Visible and the Invisible: Followed By Working Notes*? It is true that he insists on the impossibility of defining this ontology prior to the actual carrying out of his project and that he staunchly refuses to specify in advance either the nature of the inquiry or even its methodology – except to say what his interrogation 'must not be' and to caution that it 'requires a complete reconstruction of philosophy'. The notion of 'flesh', which 'has no name in any philosophy', is to be central in this reconstruction. Despite a note suggesting that his prospective definition of ontology would restrict the latter to an elaboration of key notions while that of philosophy would include the consideration of philosophy's own procedure, the bulk of Merleau-Ponty's unfinished manuscript and notes dealing with his intended ontology makes no such distinction between it and philosophy.[29] Notwithstanding his resolve to avoid any predetermination of its contours, moreover, those writings do in fact indicate that the intent of Merleau-Ponty's mature ontology-philosophy is of a piece with that of his earlier *Phenomenology*.

In light of the manifest impossibility of *compartmentalizing* Merleau-Ponty's philosophy into segments labelled, respectively, 'phenomenology', 'metaphysics' and 'ontology', we are unable to discount his final fragmentary 'ontology' as irrelevant for an assessment of his 'phenomenology' of perception, or to dismiss as inaccurate Merleau-Ponty's own assertion – made in one of his 'Working Notes' – that the *Phenomenology* 'is in fact ontology'.[30] No matter how tempting it might be to do so, it thus becomes impossible to argue, for example, that Merleau-Ponty's conception of phenomenology's proper task confines phenomenology to a description of the perceptual world, whilst metaphysics or ontology rightly probes the Being which is its source. The various passages which have been cited show, on the contrary, that we are dealing with an integral, existential philosophy. *When judged on its own terms, this philosophy consequently proves to be insufficiently radical in the Phenomenology of Perception.* The very notion of perception already suggests distinctions beyond 'our brute or wild experience' – such as that between seeing and thinking. If it is to be truly radical, the description of our lived, or 'primitive', experience must go back to what is given to us originally 'in an experience-source'.[31]

But how are we to accomplish such a return to genuinely 'brute' experience? Are we not perforce condemned to draw those minimal distinctions which philosophical inquiry itself implies? As Merleau-Ponty acknowledges, not even the most radical reflection can recapture immediate experience *as such* – for that would require a coincidence, a fusion, which reflection itself precludes. The experience to which reflection returns is inevitably an experience mediated by that very reflection. Radical, or 'concrete', philosophy is thus a profoundly paradoxical undertaking.[32] This does not mean, however, that it is of its very nature doomed to failure or that it constitutes a futile endeavour. Indeed – ironically enough – it is its own paradoxicalness which provides reflection with the requisite key to penetrate the sedimentation of acquired significances so as to elucidate the very genesis of meaning in the paradoxical nature of our lived inherence in Being. To appreciate that the *Phenomenology*'s failure to trace meaning to its origin in our self-sensing hold on brute Being is indeed a shortcoming, it is important to indicate how such a radicalized inquiry might proceed.

A rectification of the *Phenomenology*'s descriptive analysis could well take the latter's conclusion as its own point of departure. We have seen that Merleau-Ponty's phenomenological description of temporality as primordially self-aware, self-affecting subjectivity, reveals the structure of presence; and that his subsequent investigation of freedom involves an extensive critique of the Sartrian opposition between being and nothingness. That critique leads Merleau-Ponty to conclude that we must from the start be aware of being somehow centred outside ourselves, that we are not inaccessible subjectivities but rather, an intersubjective 'field of presence' and that our freedom does not consist in a secreting of nothingness, but in a transformatory exchange with what *is*. If, like Sartre, we then examine our philosophical interrogation itself, we will find that questioning does indeed define our very being; nonetheless, we will go beyond Sartre's account by exposing – as in the *Phenomenology* – the tacit presupposition in his contention that the fundamental relation which reveals itself in any question is one of rupture and opposition. Instead, we will see that the 'encounter between "us" and "what is" – these words being taken as simple indexes of a meaning to be specified' – is one of presence in which our very openness upon what is, testifies to our primordial bond with it and brings to light a common 'flesh'. Reflection on our philosophical inquiry will disclose that primary coiling or folding over, which installs us beyond ourselves in what is, and allows a novel significance to emerge in the hollow which that reflecting creates.[33]

Our reflection necessarily rests on language; yet it thrusts us out of the already established significances so that – in authentic philosophizing – we experience the coming to articulation of mute Being within our own philosophical discourse, in our very attempt to regain contact with immediate experience. In endeavouring to disclose and describe the miraculous birth of meaning in pre-reflective experience, reflection so to speak bends back over that experience and, in failing to fuse with it, creates the opening which enables the same miracle to occur in philosophical expression itself. This paradox at the core of philosophy's creativity mirrors that of our overall being-in-the-world; hence our reflection on the former can re-awaken us to an appreciation of the nature of our primordial presence to brute Being. Authentic philosophical expression emerges in the flesh of language from the 'pregnant silence' which is its invisible infrastructure and, in crystallizing into speech, takes its place in the world of already acquired significances. The transformatory exchange between the latter and the as-yet mute intention, restructures the linguistic field so that it becomes the springboard for further acts of expression. Thus philosophical inquiry interrogates Being from within and, in doing so, continually establishes new relationships with it. In general, then, the 'self-sensing' character of our own flesh opens us to what is and links us with it, while enabling us to thrust up new significances which reshape the primary given and, in turn, draw us on to ever fresh efforts of expression.

In failing to focus on this chiasma of the visible and the invisible, this intersecting of our flesh and that of brute Being, the *Phenomenology* ultimately misses the dimension of nascent meaning and thus falls short of Merleau-Ponty's express intention to offer a truly radical description. Nevertheless, its failure to uncover the very roots of our lived experience does not annul the work's worth or render it incapable of providing the sort of foundation suggested in our consideration of its contemporary relevance. It does, however, mean that philosophical reflection must coil back over the 'phenomenological' description of perception so as to push itself beyond the latter's results to a genuinely radical articulation of our paradoxical presence to what is.

The foregoing has suggested that although the *Phenomenology of Perception* constitutes a very significant advance in phenomenological–existential philosophy, it does not go far enough in describing the primordial experience which antedates all our traditional distinctions and theories. This insufficient radicalization is the *Phenomenology*'s central weakness; nonetheless, the work's additional, far less serious, shortcomings must now also be considered. The first is not actually a defect in so far as it has to do with the very nature of 'concrete' philosophy – namely, its descriptive character. As we saw earlier, Merleau-Ponty himself alerts his readers to this matter and points out that those who are firmly committed to the classical approaches will find his account confused, unconvincing and philosophically insignificant. Their own theoretical constructs will strike such critics as infinitely more real than the phenomena of experience described in the *Phenomenology*. The latter's fluid concepts will deem incomprehensible to them and, despite Merleau-Ponty's denial, they will deem simply a product of idiosyncratic introspection the ambiguous domain which he protrays. These readers will dismiss his conditional certainty, perspectival truth and pre-reflective bodily knowledge as not being any certainty, truth or knowledge at all.

Merleau-Ponty cannot counter such allegations by bringing forward some definitive experiment, unchallengeable fact, telling argument or clever proof. From the perspective of 'concrete' philosophy, these conventional rejoinders are predicated on an acceptance of the scientific preconception of the universe and the concomitant ideal of knowledge. The rebuttals are therefore themselves thoroughly uncritical. Concrete philosophy criticizes this presupposed adherence to an objective, unambiguous, precisely knowable world; consequently, it must forego the philosophical tactics which are based on what it considers to be a prejudice. Having rejected on principle the possibility of philosophical refutation, Merleau-Ponty's only recourse – as he readily acknowledges – is to endeavour to re-awaken his critics to their own experience and induce them to abandon their assumptions by disclosing the plethora of previously incomprehensible phenomena made accessible through his approach.

This sole resort is unfortunately even more problematic than Merleau-Ponty declares it to be. After all, the dogmatic readers will doubtless regard the *Phenomenology*'s description of those phenomena as more – not less – unintelligible than the traditional accounts, notwithstanding the latters' lacunae. Buttressed by both common sense and science in their belief in the objective world, such critics can hardly be expected to render themselves sufficiently present to the text so as to enable them to find Merleau-Ponty's position genuinely convincing. Given their protracted adhesion to 'the natural attitude to things' and the requisite habitual tailoring of their own experience accordingly, how are those readers to distinguish their 'actual' experience from its customary distortion? Furthermore, in light of the enormous prestige of science and the consequent pressures to discredit any experience that fails to fit the tacitly prescribed framework, what is to prompt them to suspend that 'natural attitude' which conforms with the basic assumptions of science? Why should they question the validity of long established criteria for judging reality? Why should they renounce the usual recourse to auxiliary hypothesis to rectify any alleged inadequacies in the traditional theories? Why should they consider the *Phenomenology*'s account of experience to be more inclusive than the renditions offered by the classical approaches – why not simply bring forward phenomena and experiments which the *Phenomenology* does not discuss? What is to prevent readers from reversing Merleau-Ponty's charge that they are the victims of 'a kind of mental blindness',[34] by retorting that on the contrary, *his* stubborn rejection of distinctions supported not only by common sense but also by science, evidently stems from a peculiar mental blindspot? Why not add – for good measure – that despite his insistence on the contingency of reflection, Merleau-Ponty's failure to examine the concrete origin of his *own* thought unfortunately keeps him from discovering his glaring intellectual block?!

Merleau-Ponty calls the traditional modes of philosophizing into question; hence, he lacks any *recognized* recourse against the criticisms of those who refuse to dispense with the established ways of doing and assessing philosophy. It is of little avail to declare experience the final judge and to inventory phenomena which pass the test of experience, if detractors persist in disputing the nature of that experience or challenging the credentials of this 'judge'. In the absence of all the classic philosophical comebacks to the various objections, Merleau-Ponty must supply more than the few scattered comments which he proffers regarding the character of his approach. If those who are not already committed to such a mode of philosophizing are to be induced to suspend their preconceptions sufficiently so as to heed their own underlying experience – as Merleau-Ponty evidently hopes – then the inherent difficulty in what has come to be known as 'shifting paradigms' must be addressed directly and treated in considerably greater detail than it has been in the *Phenomenology*. In addition, the readers must be alerted to their own role in accomplishing such a shift of their entire philosophical framework.

If he is to succeed in re-awakening his readers from their 'dogmatic slumber' – to use Kant's famous phrase – Merleau-Ponty must preface his 'phenomenological' description of perception with a discussion of the relationship between the reader and the text. This would induce the readers of the *Phenomenology* to reflect at the outset on their own function in disclosing the phenomena which the text describes. Having been duly sensitized to various ways of approaching a philosophical work, they would be more apt to recognize and to bracket their assumptions instead of automatically discrediting whatever resists the usual categorizations. As it is, Merleau-Ponty's brief remarks about taking up and rethinking Descartes' thought as embodied in the latter's writings, implicitly point in the direction of a fuller discussion of reading – but Merleau-Ponty fails to provide it.[35] Nor does it suffice to discuss the nature of bodily expression and comprehension, as he presents it in the *Phenomenology*, without focusing specifically on the question of how to read the text. In the absence of such an examination, Merleau-Ponty's sparse comments about the impossibility of producing proofs to support his description are likely to have very little impact on his readers. To make matters worse, Merleau-Ponty warns his readers that there can be no conclusive experiment because all experiments involve interpretations which already colour their conclusions; yet he himself occasionally makes use of experimental findings – such as those of Nagel, Stratton and Wertheimer – in a way that would suggest precisely the opposite, by speaking as if the results definitively authorize his own conclusions. Whilst there can be no question of *dispelling* the problems attending any philosophy which criticizes the established modes of thinking instead of philosophizing from within the traditional framework, a thorough exposition of those problems and a concomitant consideration of the readers' task, would go a long way in encouraging those who are wedded to the classical approaches to relinquish their tenacious hold – at least enough to appreciate the import of Merleau-Ponty's description of perception. Regrettably, the *Phenomenology* fails to offer such crucial assistance.

The requisite discussion of the relationship of the reader to the text could consist of a development of some key points of Sartre's study of literature. For example, Sartre contends in *What is Literature?* that reading is neither a mechanical registering nor an impartial contemplation of marks printed on paper. Thus if one were to read each word of a text separately, its meaning would fail to emerge because the latter is not the sum of words but rather, the organic whole. Writing and reading are dialectically correlated and constitute the two moments of what is effectively a joint venture. In seeking to disclose some truth, the prose-writer embarks on a project of communication which requires the reader's participation for its realization. Only writing and reading *together* can bring it about that something is revealed, as a revelation is only such *for* someone. Consequently, the writer implicitly appeals for the reader's collaboration. In order to comply, the reader must go beyond a merely 'abstract consciousness' of what the writer is saying. Reading is therefore 'directed creation'; but the reader is

free to reject the writer's appeal by refusing to take part. Such a
refusal prevents the text from actually becoming a disclosure – at
least as far as that reader is concerned. As Sartre puts it, 'to write is
thus both to disclose the world and to offer it as a task to the
generosity of the reader'.[36] Undoubtedly, Merleau-Ponty's development of these themes would have differed significantly from
their presentation in *What is Literature?*; in themselves, however,
they are in keeping with the description of perception in the *Phenomenology*. If the latter is to achieve its stated objective of re-
awakening the reader to an appreciation of the lived experience
subtending both the 'natural attitude' and all the theoretical
reconstructions of the world, then – despite Merleau-Ponty's evident presumption to the contrary – that study cannot in fact
dispense with an explicit examination of the sort of themes
outlined here.

Merleau-Ponty's recurrent heavy reliance on the results of
studies dealing with pathological behaviour – particularly those
of Goldstein and Gelb pertaining to Schneider – also considerably
weakens his description of perception. In the absence of any
adequate discussion of the difficulties inherent in the very nature
of his philosophy and the kind of approach which its comprehension requires on the part of the reader, it is especially tempting for
the latter to dismiss the *Phenomenology*. The grounds for such
dismissal might well be that Schneider's experience proves nothing because it is too individual and in any case, too different to
throw any possible light on normal experience. Further, the reader
might challenge the conclusions stemming from Merleau-Ponty's
assessment of Schneider's reported behaviour, by arguing that
they are mere theoretical constructions of alleged experience and
that Merleau-Ponty is himself guilty of tailoring observations to
fit his own preconceptions concerning the nature of our normal
experience. The reader can thus simply level at Merleau-Ponty
the latter's own charge against the classical theorists – that they
are fundamentally uncritical in their interpretation of human
experience.

To forestall such objections, Merleau-Ponty would need to
discuss in much greater detail the meaning of 'facts', 'data' and
observations; the philosophical status of experiments; the issue of
interpretation and his own use of experimental findings. For him,
of course, it is not a matter of *proving* anything but rather, of
describing the phenomena as he sees them upon putting his

'natural attitude' in abeyance. Ultimately, his readers must judge
for themselves whether that description adequately captures the
lived structures of their own pre-reflective experience. In order to
be in a position to make that judgement, however, they must first
re-awaken to an awareness of their actual experience. Given the
difficulty of achieving such awareness, Merleau-Ponty quite
rightly examines behavioural breakdowns to draw attention to
their normal counterpart. After all, the recognition of illness
already implies a conception of health; hence, a close consideration of the former can indeed bring to light the unacknowledged
preconceptions in the latter, thereby enabling us to put those aside
and *see* our experience as it really is. It is unfortunate, therefore,
that Merleau-Ponty has not supplied the necessary methodological
discussion for this approach.

Merleau-Ponty's method in the *Phenomenology* clearly also involves a continual juxtaposition of the 'empiricist' and 'intellectualist' approaches; consequently, it is essential to consider
whether that perpetual juxtaposition in any way weakens the
Phenomenology. On first consideration, it may seem that Merleau-
Ponty has erected straw pins whose toppling requires little effort,
for neither position is *consistently* identifiable with the works of
any *single* philosopher or psychologist. This does not mean,
however, that either of these positions is an artificially created
stance. Merleau-Ponty's own references to various writings,
supplemented by the sources cited and discussed in this exegesis,
indicate that the positions are by no means artificial – although
they *are* extreme. Nonetheless, it might still be argued that few of
today's philosophers adopt such positions, most preferring to take
a less extreme, more flexible stand. That may indeed be the case;
yet it does not follow that Merleau-Ponty's critique of 'empiricism'
and 'intellectualism' thereby loses its force and becomes merely of
historical interest. We must remember that Merleau-Ponty also
discusses hybrids of the two positions and shows that they share
the same basic assumptions; moreover, in the *Phenomenology* we
have seen the same fundamental prejudice underlying both extremes. Despite their apparent difference, the majority of existing
approaches continue to rest on that bias.

There is nevertheless a sense in which Merleau-Ponty's persi-
stent focus on 'empiricism' and 'intellectualism' does indeed
weaken his description of perception. His manner of presenting
and criticizing the extremes frequently makes it exceedingly

difficult to discern Merleau-Ponty's own position on the particular issue under consideration. More importantly, his preoccupation with 'empiricism' and 'intellectualism' is no doubt at least partially responsible for the relative lack in development of his own position. The bulk of his efforts is devoted to exposing the inadequacies of the traditional approaches, thereby frequently leaving his response beyond their critique largely a matter of implication. As a result, Merleau-Ponty's own key concepts receive far too little elaboration and the issues which he addresses remain very undeveloped. There is all too little discussion, for example, of the meaning of notions such as field, horizon, ambiguity, certainty, truth, rationality, comprehension, knowledge, fact, 'value-fact', motivation, sedimentation, necessity, contingency, intentionality, power, nature, culture, 'interworld', significance and 'meaning' itself. This is most unfortunate, as Merleau-Ponty indicates that we are not simply to assign their usual meanings to these pivotal terms. Nor is his own use of them always entirely consistent – especially in the case of 'meaning', 'significance', 'nature' and 'culture'. A number of crucial questions regarding the meanings, import and interrelations of the various notions thus remain unanswered in the text. For example, Merleau-Ponty's own use of the terms 'nature' and 'culture' is sometimes very narrow – yet occasionally quite broad. His remarks about the primacy of perception, as well as the approach which he actually employs in describing it in the *Phenomenology*, would suggest that there is a level of 'culture' *above* the level of perception and that the fundamental structures of the latter can be elucidated whilst bracketing any consideration of the former. Yet as Merleau-Ponty himself acknowledges at various points, it is ultimately impossible to maintain a distinction between 'nature' and 'culture' and to consider them as 'lower' or 'higher' layers, respectively.

It would seem that our perception is always already imbued with 'cultural' meanings and values, so that it is in fact misleading to imply that we can examine perception without at the same time investigating questions of 'rationality' and 'values'. As Merleau-Ponty's own discussion of expression and speech indicates, our perception is inherently laden with 'cultural' influences. Just as the question of what the world was like before the appearance of humans, is meaningless and a world without a human perspective inconceivable, the question of the being of bodily experience anterior to any cultural influence is also meaningless, and the absence of the latter inconceivable. This would suggest that bodily experience cannot be adequately studied in abstraction from the belonging of the body-subject to a particular culture; hence, the description of perception might well need to be much more culturally specific than Merleau-Ponty's description in fact is. There can be no question of resolving this extremely complex issue here; nevertheless, it must at least be noted that even the notion of 'perception' is not adequately considered in the *Phenomenology*. Then too, there are broader questions which remain substantially unresolved in the text – such as the meaning and implications of an absolute within the relativity of our experience, or the parameters of this sort of philosophy and the need for a much more radical departure from the traditional philosophical terminology in order to articulate the novelty of approach. On the other hand, it is important to keep in mind that Merleau-Ponty at no time considered his *Phenomenology* to constitute a definitive statement; on the contrary, he explicitly asserted his intention to undertake subsequently the necessary studies of 'culture', language, intersubjectivity, philosophy, truth and the like.[37] In his own eyes, therefore, the *Phenomenology* was a preliminary investigation whose various themes were to be pursued in more depth upon its completion. As we have seen, those subsequent studies were never finished. Consequently, the many questions which the *Phenomenology* implicitly raises but leaves unanswered, call all the more urgently on the readers' own resources to take up and carry forward Merleau-Ponty's uncompleted inquiry. In its sustained attempt to re-awaken its readers to the enigmatic richness of their own lived experience, the description of perception provides the requisite tools for embarking on such an endeavour. Despite its preliminary nature, its lacunae and insufficient radicality, Merleau-Ponty's *Phenomenology of Perception* thus makes a very substantial contribution to the philosophical discourse of our time.

Notes

1. *Phenomenology of Perception*, xvii–xviii.
2. G. W. F. Hegel, *The Phenomenology of Mind* (trans. J. B. Baillie), (New York: Harper & Row, 1967), pp. 162–3, 177, 800ff.
3. Heidegger, 'Letter on Humanism', *The Existentialist Tradition: Selected Writings*, p. 229.
4. Ibid., p. 233.
5. See, for example, Kierkegaard, *The Present Age* (trans. Alexander Dru), (New York: Harper & Row, 1962) pp. 56ff., 62; Kierkegaard, *Fear and Trembling* and *The Sickness Unto Death* (trans. Walter Lowrie), (New York: Doubleday & Co., 1954) pp. 30ff., 208ff.; Jaspers, *Reason and Existenz* (trans. William Earle), (New York: Noonday Press, 1955) pp. 51–77, 137ff.; Marcel, *The Philosophy of Existentialism* (trans. Manya Harari), (New York: Citadel Press, 1966) pp 15ff., 46, 94ff.
6. *Being and Nothingness: a Phenomenological Essay on Ontology*, pp. 126, 377, 472–7, 555, 568–70, 617, 647, 651–7, 671–4, 784, 797.
7. 'The Phenomenal Field', *Phenomenology of Perception*, pp. 56–7.
8. Merleau-Ponty's notion of 'value-fact' is a modality of that mediating 'third term' which is lacking, for example, in Sartre's analysis of our being-in-the-world. It challenges – so it seems to me – Sartre's strict demarcation between ontology and ethics. (See, for example, *Being and Nothingness: a Phenomenological Essay on Ontology*, p. 795.)
9. 'The Primacy of Perception and Its Philosophical Consequences', *The Primacy of Perception and Other Essays*, pp. 25–6. See also p. 39 regarding Merleau-Ponty's refusal to separate his phenomenological description from his conclusions pertaining to the practical realm.
10. *Phenomenology of Perception*, p. 127.
11. Ibid., p. 179.
12. Merleau-Ponty, *The Visible and the Invisible: Followed by Working Notes* (ed. Claude Lefort and trans. Alphonso Lingis), Evanston: Northwestern University Press, 1968) p. 200.
13. Ibid., p. 200. (Note that Merleau-Ponty is not consistent in capitalizing 'Being' and '*Logos*'. Occasionally, as in this case, he fails to do so.)
14. *Phenomenology of Perception*, p. 197.
15. Ibid., vii, xiv, xv, xx, xxi.
16. *The Visible and the Invisible: Followed by Working Notes*, p. 168.
17. *La prose du monde* (ed. Claude Lefort), (Paris: Gallimard, 1969); English translation by John O'Neill, *The Prose of the World* (Evanston, Ill.: Northwestern University Press, 1973). For a discussion of the relationship between this work and Merleau-Ponty's *The Visible and the Invisible*, see Claude Lefort's 'Avertissement'/ 'Introduction' to the former. His 'Foreward' to *The Visible and the Invisible* is also very helpful, as is the 'Translator's Preface'.
18. 'Eye and Mind', *The Primacy of Perception and Other Essays*, p. 159. As the translator notes, this essay was the final work published in Merleau-Ponty's own lifetime. It first appeared in Jan. 1961.

19. 'Working Notes', *The Visible and the Invisible: Followed by Working Notes*, pp. 170–1, 175–6, 178–9.

20. *The Visible and the Invisible: Followed by Working Notes*, pp. 138–40, 146, 167, 170, 202–3, 224, 250–1.

21. Ibid., pp. 185, 215–6.

22. For a very useful 'sketch' of Merleau-Ponty's philosophy of language, see James M. Edie's 'Forward' to *Consciousness and the Acquisition of Language* by Merleau-Ponty, translated by Hugh Silverman (Evanston, Ill.: Northwestern University Press, 1973) pp. xi–xxxii. Once again, the 'Translator's Preface' is also helpful.

23. 'Working Notes', *The Visible and the Invisible: Followed by Working Notes*, 202–3.

24. 'Preface', *Phenomenology of Perception*, pp. vii–ix, xiii–xv.

25. Ibid., xiv, xvii–xix.

26. 'The Film and the New Psychology', *Sense and Non-Sense* (trans. Hubert L. Dreyfus and Patricia A. Dreyfus), (Evanston, Ill.: Northwestern University Press, 1964), p. 58.

27. 'Marxism and Philosophy', *Sense and Non-Sense*, pp. 133–4; 'The Metaphysical in Man', *Sense and Non-Sense*, pp. 92–8. Merleau-Ponty's 1961 lecture notes on 'philosophy and non-philosophy' testify to his unflagging concern that philosophy be 'concrete'. See, for example, 'Merleau-Ponty: Philosophie et non-philosophie depuis Hegel – Notes de cours (II)', *Textures*, 10–11, 1975, pp. 163–4.

28. Merleau-Ponty, 'Introduction', *Signs* (trans. Richard C. McClearly), (Evanston, Ill.: Northwestern University Press, 1964) pp. 20–2, 157–8.

29. *The Visible and the Invisible: Followed by Working Notes*, pp. 139, 147, 158–9, 167, 179, 193, 259.

30. Ibid., p. 176.

31. Ibid., pp. 158–62.

32. Ibid., pp. 35ff., 44–6, 102, 122–9, 158–62, 174, 197.

33. A close reading of *The Visible and the Invisible: Followed by Working Notes* suggests that Merleau-Ponty intended to take the sort of approach which I have outlined to radicalize his earlier description of perception. See, for example, pp. 31ff., 50–95, 99–104, 119–29, 156–62, 197. See also the 'Introduction', *Signs*, pp. 14–22.

34. *Phenomenology of Perception*, p. 25.

35. The following cursory remarks which Merleau-Ponty makes in his chapter on 'The Cogito' are especially interesting for a discussion of the relationship between the text and its reader: 'This book, once begun, is not a certain set of ideas; it constitutes for me an open situation, for which I could not possibly provide any complex formula, and in which I struggle blindly on until, miraculously, thoughts and words become organized by themselves.' (*Phenomenology of Perception*, p. 369) *and*: 'It is I who reconstitute the historical *cogito*, I who read Descartes' text, I who recognize in it an undying truth, so that finally the Cartesian *cogito* acquires its [meaning] only through my own *cogito* . . .' (Ibid., p. 371).

36. Sartre, *What is Literature?* (trans. Bernard Frechtman), (London: Methuen, 1950) pp. 10–13, 29–32, 39–44, 51. Note that a crucial

phrase is missing on p. 30 of this translation. The French original reads: 'Aussi les cent mille mots alignés dans un livre peuvent être lus un à un sans que les sens de l'œuvre en jaillisse; le sens n'est pas la somme des mots, il en est la totalité organique.' (Sartre, *Qu'est-ce que la littérature?* (Paris: Gallimard, 1948) p.56.) As we might expect, there are a number of fundamental points in Sartre's *What is Literature?* which are at odds with Merleau-Ponty's position. In fact, Sartre refers to the *Phenomenology* in his opening pages and explicitly rejects the notion that there is any parallelism between literature on the one hand, and the art of the painter, sculptor or musician on the other. Merleau-Ponty, for his part, evinced substantial disagreement with Sartre's book and intended to undertake a detailed study of literature in reply. Unfortunately, that project did not materialize beyond his unfinished manuscript *The Prose of the World* and the essays on language. In any case, such a detailed treatment would – obviously – have been too late and too long for incorporation into the *Phenomenology*. What the latter sorely lacks, however, is at least *some* explicit consideration of its readers' relationship to the text – somewhat along the lines I have indicated. (Those points *do* harmonize with the *Phenomenology*.) For further consideration, see the first two pages of Sartre's *What is Literature?*, as well as Claude Lefort's 'Avertissement' to *La prose du monde* (vii–viii) and Bernard Pingaud's article 'Merleau-Ponty, Sartre et la littérature', *L'ARC*, no. 46 (1971) pp. 80–8.

37 'An Unpublished Text by Maurice Merleau-Ponty: a Prospectus of His Work', *The Primacy of Perception*, pp. 3–11.

Bibliography

Please Note: As my book is directed primarily at English speaking readers, I am listing the English translations of works when these are available, rather than the original texts.

Berman, Morris, 'The Cybernetic Dream of the 21st Century'. Paper presented at 'An International Conference on Social and Technological Change: The University into the 21st Century', University of Victoria, British Columbia, Canada, 4 May 1984.

Chappell, V. C. (ed.), *The Philosophy of Mind* (Englewood Cliffs, N.J.: Prentice-Hall, Inc., 1962).

Descartes, R., *Meditations on First Philosophy* in *Philosophical Writings* (trans. and eds Elizabeth Anscombe and Peter Thomas Geach), (London: Thomas Nelson and Sons Ltd., Nelson's University Paperbacks for The Open University, 1970).

Edie, James M., 'Forward', *Consciousness and the Acquisition of Language* by Merleau-Ponty (trans. Hugh Silverman and ed. James M. Edie), (Evanston, Ill.: Northwestern University Press, 1973).

Guerrière, Daniel, 'Table of Contents of "Phenomenology of Perception:" Translation and Pagination', *Journal of the British Society for Phenomenology*, vol. 10, no. 1 (Jan. 1979).

Hegel, G. W. F., *The Phenomenology of Mind* (trans. J. B. Baillie), (New York: Harper & Row, 1967).

Heidegger, Martin, *Being and Time* (trans. John Macquarrie and Edward Robinson), (London: S.C.M. Press, 1962; Library of Philosophy and Theology).

Heidegger, Martin, 'Letter on Humanism' (trans. Edgar Lohner) in *The Existentialist Tradition: Selected Writings* (ed. Nino Langiulli), (New York: Doubleday, 1971).

Heidegger, Martin, 'Memorial Address', *Discourse on Thinking* (trans. Anderson and Freund), (New York: Harper & Row, 1969).

Husserl, Edmund, *The Idea of Phenomenology* (trans. William P. Alston and George Nakhnikian), (The Hague: Martinus Nijhoff, 1964).

Husserl, Edmund, *The Phenomenology of Internal Time-Consciousness* (ed. Martin Heidegger and trans. James S. Churchill), (Indiana University Press, 1964).

Husserl, Edmund, *Ideas: General Introduction to Pure Phenomenology* (trans. W. R. Boyce Gibson), (London: Collier-Macmillan, 1962).

Husserl, Edmund, *Phenomenology and the Crisis of Philosophy: Philosophy as Rigorous Science* and *Philosophy and the Crisis of European Man* (trans. Quentin Lauer), (New York: Harper & Row, 1965).

Husserl, Edmund, *Cartesian Meditations: an Introduction to Phenomenology* (trans. Dorion Cairns), (The Hague, Martinus Nijhoff, 1960).

Jaspers, Karl, *The Future of Mankind* (trans. E. B. Ashton), (University of Chicago Press, 1961).

Jaspers, Karl, *Man in the Modern Age* (trans. Eden & Cedar Paul), (New York: Doubleday, 1957).

Jaspers, Karl, 'Philosophizing Starts with Our Situation'. *Philosophy*, vol. I (trans. E. B. Ashton) in *The Existentialist Tradition: Selected Writings*.

Jaspers, Karl, *Reason and Existenz* (trans. William Earle), (New York: Noonday Press, 1955).

Kant, I., 'Introduction'. *Critique of Pure Reason* (trans. Norman Kemp Smith), (New York: St. Martin's Press, 1965).

Kierkegaard, S., *Fear and Trembling* and *The Sickness Unto Death* (trans. Walter Lowrie), (New York: Doubleday & Co., 1954).

Kierkegaard, S., *The Present Age* (trans. Alexander Dru), (New York: Harper & Row, 1962).

Kockelmans, Joseph J. (ed.), *Phenomenology: the Philosophy of Edmund Husserl and Its Interpretation* (New York: Doubleday, 1967).

Lefort, Claude, 'Introduction'. *The Prose of the World* by Merleau-Ponty (trans. John O'Neill), (Evanston, Ill.: Northwestern University Press, 1973).

Lefort, Claude, 'Forward', *The Visible and the Invisible: Followed by Working Notes* by Merleau-Ponty (trans. Alphonso Lingis and ed. Claude Lefort), (Evanston, Ill.: Northwestern University Press, 1968).

Lingis, Alphonso, 'Translator's Preface', *The Visible and the Invisible: Followed by Working Notes*.

Marcel, Gabriel, *The Philosophy of Existentialism* (trans. Manya Harari), (New York: Citadel Press, 1966).

Merleau-Ponty, Maurice, *Phenomenology of Perception* (trans. Colin Smith), (London: Routledge & Kegan Paul, 1961; repr. with translation revisions 1981).

Merleau-Ponty, Maurice, 'Merleau-Ponty: Philosophie et non-philosophie depuis Hegel – Notes de cours (II)', *Textures*, 10–11 (1975).

Merleau-Ponty, Maurice, 'Eye and Mind', 'An Unpublished Text By Maurice Merleau-Ponty: a Prospectus of His Work', 'The Primacy of Perception and Its Philosophical Consequences'. *The Primacy of Perception and Other Essays* (ed. James M. Edie), (Evanston, Ill.: Northwestern University Press, 1964).

Merleau-Ponty, Maurice, *Signs* (trans. Richard C. McCleary), (Evanston, Ill.: Northwestern University Press, 1964).

Merleau-Ponty, Maurice, *The Visible and the Invisible: Followed by Working Notes* (trans. Alphonso Lingis and ed. Claude Lefort), (Evanston, Ill.: Northwestern University Press, 1968).

Merleau-Ponty, Maurice, 'The War Has Taken Place', 'Marxism and Philosophy', 'The Metaphysical in Man', 'The Film and the New Psychology'. *Sense and Non-Sense* (trans. Hubert L. Dreyfus and Patricia A. Dreyfus), (Evanston, Ill.: Northwestern University Press, 1964).

Merleau-Ponty, Maurice, *Adventurers of the Dialectic* (trans. Joseph Bien), (Evanston, Ill.: Northwestern University Press, 1973).

Merleau-Ponty, Maurice, *The Prose of the World* (trans. John O'Neill), (Evanston, Ill.: Northwestern University Press, 1973).

Pingaud, Bernard, 'Merleau-Ponty, Sartre et la littérature'. *L'ARC*, no.46 (1971).

Ryle, Gilbert, *The Concept of Mind* (Harmondsworth, Middlesex: Penguin, 1976).

Sartre, Jean-Paul, *Being and Nothingness: a Phenomenological Essay on Ontology* (trans. Hazel Barnes), (New York: Washington Square Press, 1966).

Sartre, Jean-Paul, *The Emotions: Outline of a Theory* (trans. Bernard Frechtman), (New York: Philosophical Library, 1948).

Sartre, Jean-Paul, *The Transcendence of the Ego: An Existentialist Theory of Consciousness* (trans. Forrest Williams and Robert Kirkpatrick), (New York: Noonday Press, 1957).

Sartre, Jean-Paul, *What is Literature?* (trans. Bernard Frechtman), (London: Methuen, 1950).

INDEX